NATURAL HISTORY

OF THE

INSECTS OF INDIA

NATURAL HISTORY
OF THE
INSECTS OF INDIA,

CONTAINING

UPWARDS OF TWO HUNDRED AND TWENTY

FIGURES AND DESCRIPTIONS,

BY

E. DONOVAN, F.L.S. & W.S.

A NEW EDITION,

BY J. O. WESTWOOD

GYAN

Published by

Gyan Publishing House
5, Ansari Road
Daryaganj, New Delhi-110002
Phone: 011-47034999, 9811692060
E-mail: books@gyanbooks.com

Distribution Network
gyanbooks.com
India, USA, Canada, UK, Australia, France

ISBN: 978-81-212-8011-2 (PB)
First Published, 1842

2nd Impression 2023

Printed at: Gyan Press, Delhi.

NATURAL HISTORY OF THE INSECTS OF INDIA
Author: E. DONOVAN, Editor: J. O. WESTWOOD

Dynastes (Chalcosoma) Atlas.

NATURAL HISTORY

OF THE

INSECTS OF INDIA,

CONTAINING

UPWARDS OF TWO HUNDRED AND TWENTY

FIGURES AND DESCRIPTIONS,

BY

E. DONOVAN, F.L.S. & W.S.

A NEW EDITION,

BROUGHT DOWN TO THE PRESENT STATE OF THE SCIENCE,
WITH SYSTEMATIC CHARACTERS OF EACH SPECIES, SYNONYMS, INDEXES, AND OTHER ADDITIONAL MATTER,

BY J. O. WESTWOOD,

SECRETARY OF THE ENTOMOLOGICAL SOCIETY OF LONDON, HON. MEM. OF THE LITERARY AND HISTORICAL SOCIETY OF QUEBEC, AND OF THE NATURAL HISTORY SOCIETIES OF MOSCOW, LILLE, MAURITIUS, ETC.

LONDON:

HENRY G. BOHN, 4 & 5, YORK STREET, COVENT GARDEN.

MDCCCXLII.

PREFACE.

At the period when the first edition of this work was presented to the public, the study of exotic insects, and indeed the science of Entomology itself, had made but little progress in this country. The collections of Francillon, Drury, MacLeay, Sir J. Banks, and Donovan, contained almost all that was then known of Indian Entomology, with which our Continental neighbours were then, as still, comparatively ignorant. To these collections, examined by Fabricius himself, Donovan had free access, and his figures of the insects therein contained, which had served as types for the descriptions of the Entomologist of Kiel, are especially valuable.

The progress of Entomology, as a science, has so much advanced, as to render a republication of this work advisable; at the same time, however, requiring that its original Linnæan style should not be retained, but that it should be brought down to the present state of science. This I have endeavoured to do, by rendering the specific characters more detailed, the nomenclature more correct, the synonyms more numerous, and the localities more precise. I have added many additional observations, omitting nothing which appeared in the former at all likely to instruct or interest the reader. Alphabetical and systematic indices of the work are introduced, as well as numbers, both for the plates, and for the individual figures on each plate, which were omitted in the former edition, which appeared in parts, commencing in the year 1800.

It has unfortunately happened, from the careless indications of the older authorities, that many insects inhabiting the West Indies have been given as natives of East India; and hence it has happened that Donovan, having no means of ascertaining the true locality of various species, introduced into the present work several West Indian insects. With these exceptions, the present work is intended to illustrate "the Entomological productions of a country for which we ought to cherish the liveliest and deepest interest, as being connected intimately with the prosperity, the dignity, and the honour of the British Empire;—in a word, of British India"; embracing also illustrations of those species which inhabit every other part of that vast continent, as well as the islands situated in the Indian Seas.

In respect, therefore, both to the circumstance of this great territory being peculiarly confided to our care, and more especially to the remarkable character of its natural productions, the investigation of its Entomological treasures becomes the especial province of the English entomologist.

Thus, whilst our museums teem with undescribed insects from India, collected by General Hardwicke, Colonel Sykes, Colonel Whithill, Captain Smee, Messrs. Saunders, Royle, Downes, &c. &c., Dr. Perty, writing in 1831, observes in his "Observationes nonnullæ in Coleoptera Indiæ Orientalis,"—"Præsertim tempore novissimo in Galliæ et Germaniæ museis, communicatione propinqua cum illa regione deficiente, Indiæ orientalis Coleoptera rarius inveniuntur."

In order to shew the peculiar character of Indian Entomology to its full extent, a far greater space would be required than can here be possibly given to it. A few remarks will not, however, be out of place.

From its peculiar situation, as the great intermediate southern peninsula of Asia, it may be easily conceived, not only that India comprises various types of form peculiar to itself, but that it also borrows portions of those found in the Arabian and Siamese peninsulæ; the former of which comprises, of course, a greater portion of forms peculiar to eastern Africa, Asia minor, and even southern Turkey; whilst to the latter is imparted a portion of the peculiarities of the Entomology of Borneo, and the other great islands lying south of the Equator. The entomological peculiarities of the Himalayan Mountains have been submitted to a minute analysis, by the Rev. F. W. Hope.

In the order Coleoptera we accordingly find various genera and species, either exclusively confined to India, or occurring therein and in the countries above indicated. Thus the most splendid species of Cicindela, and the genera Therates, Tricondyla, and Colliuris, in the family Cicindelidæ, do not occur beyond the limits of India and the Indian Archipelago. The genera Catascopus, Orthogonius, many fine Panagæi, &c. amongst the Carabidæ; the most splendid of all the Buprestidæ, and the beautiful group of Elateridæ, typified by Elater aureolus, (some of the species of both of which extend in their range to China,) occur in India. In the great group of Lamellicorn Coleoptera, (Scarabæus, *Linn.*) the species of Onthophagus are excessively numerous, of large size and fine colours, whilst the giant Dynastidæ, (which are so abundant in South America,) are here represented chiefly by the small group Chalcosoma, *Hope*, (S. Atlas, &c.) and by D. Dichotomus and D. longimanus; the Cetoniæ, Euchloræ, and Popilliæ, on the other hand, are far more numerous and beautiful. The Lucani are of much larger size, and far more numerous than in South America. The species of Longicorn beetles are numerous, but the giant Prioni are of very rare occurrence in India, as compared with South America. The splendid genera Sagra, Podontia, and Phyllocharis, with many fine Eumorphi, and various Paussidæ, are especially natives of these regions.

In the Orthoptera, many curious Phasmæ, with the singular genus Phyllium, and numerous splendid Grylli, *Linn.*, including the remarkable Schizodactyla monstrosa, may be mentioned. In the Hemiptera, the most splendid of all the species of Scutellera, and of Cicada, with several curious Fulgoræ, and other Fulgorideous insects;*

* M. Guérin has recently elucidated this group, in Bélanger's "Voyage aux Indes Orientales."

and in the Lepidoptera, Priamus, and its allies, (the most magnificent of all the butterflies, *Ornithopterus*,) and the delicate Ideæ, are especially to be noticed, as well as several species of the curious Dipterous genus Diopsis.

We are still, however, far from having attained a perfect idea of the Entomological treasures of India, every new arrival making us acquainted with new and beautiful species.

INDIA.

Order. COLEOPTERA, *Linnæus.*

DYNASTES (CHALCOSOMA) ATLAS.

Plate I.

TRIBE. LAMELLICORNES, *Latreille.*

FAMILY. DYNASTIDÆ, *MacLeay.*

GENUS. DYNASTES, *MacLeay.* Scarabæus, *Latreille.* Geotrupes, *Fabricius.* (SUBGENUS: Chalcosoma, *Hope.*)

SPECIES. DYNASTES ATLAS: cupreo-niger, thorace tricorni; anteriori brevissimo; capitis cornu longissimo adscendente, in medio dente armato. Long. Corp. $3\frac{3}{4}$ unc., (absque cornu capitis).

DYNASTES: coppery black; the thorax with three horns, the central one very short; the head with a long ascending horn, with a tooth in the middle. Length of the body, without the horn of the head, $3\frac{3}{4}$ inches.

SYN. Scarabæus Atlas? *Linn. Syst. Nat. vol.* I. *pars.* 2, *p.* 542. *Mus. Lud. Reg.* 6. *Fabricius Syst. Eleuth.* I. *p.* 10, *No.* 29. *Swammerdam's Book of Nature, tab.* 30, *f.* 3. *Margr. Brazil,* 247, *f.* 1. *Merian Ins. Surinam, in title page. Edwards's Birds, tab.* 105, *f.* 1.

This is one of the most extraordinary species of the great Scarabæi of Linnæus. The specimen here figured was purchased by the late Mr. Tunstal, from the cabinet of a Dutch governor in the East Indies, with other rare species figured in this work. At the period of the first publication of this work it was considered unique, and was regarded as an inhabitant of the island of Amboyna, in the East Indies. Linnæus, Fabricius, Madame Merian, and Margrave, give South America as the locality of the insect described in the works of the two former authors under the name of Scarabæus

Atlas, whilst Swammerdam and Edwards, who are both referred to by Linnæus, give Japan and Borneo as its habitat.

That the East Indies is the real locality of the insect here represented, is rendered most probable, from the circumstance of several other, and very closely allied species, being found in that part of the world. Such are the Scarabæus Caucasus, *Fabr.* (described from an East Indian specimen in the British Museum, and regarded by Olivier, and Jablonsky, as a variety of Atlas); Scarabeus Charon, *Oliv.*; the Javanese Scarabæus Hector, *Dejean;* Dynastes Hesperus, *Erichson,* from the island of Luzon; and Dynastes Jephthah, of *MacLeay,* (in the collection of the Entomological Society). It is true that the chief distinctions amongst these species are found in the size of the horns of the head and thorax, and in the teeth, or serration of the hinder part of the horn of the head; but it is equally true, that we are by no means furnished with sufficiently accurate data for ascertaining the extent of variation in the cornuted Scarabæi in this respect, and we are therefore by no means enabled to regard these as satisfactory species. Indeed, in the volume of the Naturalist's Library devoted to exotic Coleoptera, we have an original figure of an insect, with the name of Atlas attached, in which the horn of the head has a double series of serratures from the base to the apex, and which was brought from Rangoon; and in the Fabrician description this horn is stated to be tridentate, the anterior tooth being the strongest.

As it is, however, most probable that some, at least, of the above mentioned species are distinct, it is convenient to regard these insects as forming a distinct sub-genus, characterized not only by the peculiar structure of the horns, and the polished surface of the body, but by the variations in the structure of the mouth. Mr. Hope has accordingly given to them the name of Chalcosoma, in his Coleopterous Manual, recently published.

ONTHOPHAGUS SPINIFEX.

Plate II. fig. 1.

FAMILY. SCARABÆIDÆ, *MacLeay.*

GENUS. ONTHOPHAGUS, *Latreille.* Copris p. *Fabricius.* Scarabæus p. *Linnæus.*

SPECIES. ONTHOPHAGUS SPINIFEX: thorace rotundato inermi; occipite spinâ recurvâ thoracis longitudine; thorace et elytris nigris, viridi nitidis; his striatis; pedibus nigris. Long. Corp. lin. $3\frac{1}{2}$.

ONTHOPHAGUS: with a rounded and unarmed thorax; the forehead with a recurved spine as long as the thorax; the latter, as well as the elytra, black shaded with green; the elytra striated, and the legs black. Length $3\frac{1}{2}$ lines.

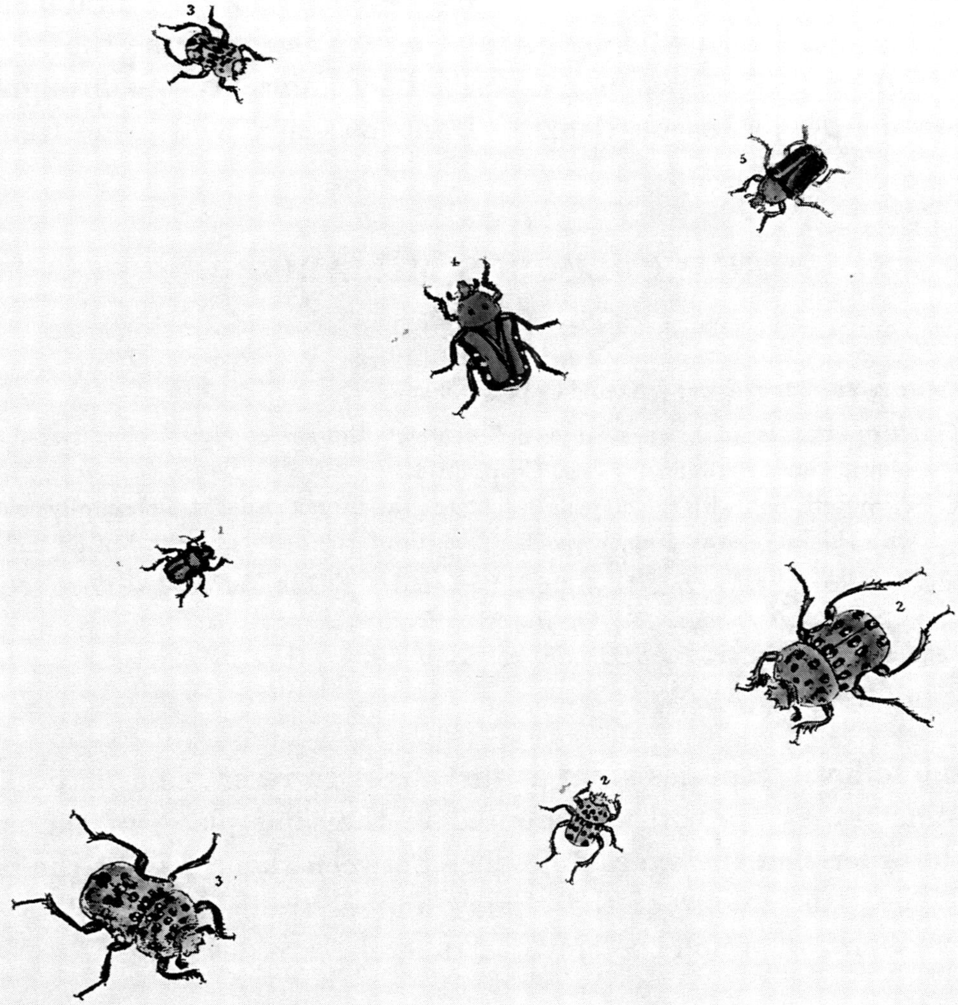

1. *Onthophagus spinifex.* 2. *Gymnopleurus miliaris.* 3.
4. *Cetonia Histrio.* 5. *Gymnetis cœrulea.*

COLEOPTERA.

Syn. Scarabæus spinifex, *Fabricius Ent. Syst.* 1. *p.* 58. *sp.* 190. *Herbst. Coleopt.* II. *p.* 240. *No.* 146. *Donovan edit.* 1, *in text.*

Scarabæus spinifer, *Oliv. Ent.* 1.3. 148. *No.* 180. *t.* 12. *f.* 112. *Donovan edit.* 1 *in tab.*

Fabricius describes this species as being of the same size as Onthophagus nuchicornis, with the occipital horn as long as the thorax, and with the thorax and elytra black tinged with green. The specimen described by Fabricius, was brought from the Coast of Coromandel by Sir Joseph Banks. Donovan's specimens were from Bengal.

GYMNOPLEURUS MILIARIS.

Plate II. fig. 2.

Genus: Gymnopleurus, *Illiger.* Ateuchus p. *Fabricius.*

Species. Gymnopleurus Miliaris: clypeo 6-dentato; thorace et elytris obscuris, maculis elevatis atris nitidulis. Long. Corp. lin 4.

Gymnopleurus: with the clypeus 6-dentate; the thorax and elytra obscurely coloured, with shining elevated black spots. Length of the body, one-third of an inch.

Syn. Scarabæus miliaris, *Oliv. Ins.* 1. 3. 167. 206. *t.* 18. *f.* 164. *Fabricius Ent. Syst.* 1. *p.* 63. *No.* 209. *Herbst. Col.* II. *p.* 322. *No.* 206.

Ateuchus miliaris, *Fabr. Syst. Eleuth. vol.* 1. *p.* 56.

Habitat. "India," (*Fabricius*).

This and the following species seem at first sight to resemble each other, but are nevertheless distinct: they are both represented in the same plate, of the natural size and magnified, in order that the exact difference between them may be the more easily discriminated. The pale colour of the thorax and elytra is produced by numerous minute incumbent hairs, of which the elevated tubercles are destitute.

GYMNOPLEURUS KŒNIGII.

Plate II. fig. 3.

Species. Gymnopleurus Kœnigii: clypeo bidentato; thorace et elytris pallidis, maculis atris elevatis nitidulis, his variolosis. Long. Corp. lin. 4.

Gymnopleurus: with the clypeus bidentate; the thorax and elytra pale, with elevated shining black spots, the latter variolose, with some of the spots confluent. Length of the body, 4 lines.

Syn. Scarabæus Kœnigii, *Oliv. Ins.* 1. 3. 163. 200. *t.* 9, *f.* 77. *Fabricius Ent. Syst.* 1, *p.* 65. *Herbst. Col.* II. *p.* 300, *No.* 195, *t.* 19, *f.* 8.
Scarabæus scriptus, *Pallas Icon. p.* 7. *A.* 7. *T. A. f.* 7.

Fabricius gives Tranquebar as the locality of this species. I have seen it in some collections named Gymnopleurus granulatus, which Fabricius, indeed, regarded as a variety of Gymnopleurus Kœnigii.

CETONIA HISTRIO.

Plate II. fig. 4.

Family. Cetoniadæ, *MacLeay.*

Genus. Cetonia, *Fabricius.* Scarabæus p. *Linnæus.*

Species. Cetonia Histrio: testacea; thorace maculis duabus nigris; elytris nigris, singulo macula magna oblonga testacea, punctisque quatuor lateralibus albis. Long. Corp. lin. 8.

Cetonia: testaceous; thorax with two black spots; elytra black, each having a large oblong testaceous spot, and four lateral small round white spots. Length 8 lines.

Syn. Cetonia histrio, *Oliv. Hist. Ins.* 1. 6. 45, *tab.* 10, *f.* 94. *Fabricius Ent. Syst.* 2. 152.
Cetonia versicolor, *Oliv. Fabr. var.? Schonh. Syn. Ins.* 1. 3, *p.* 131.

Habitat. Egypt, (*Fabricius*). Egypt, and East Indies, (*Schonherr*). Bengal, (*Mus. Hope*).

GYMNETIS CÆRULEA.

Plate II. fig. 5.

Genus. Gymnetis, *MacLeay.* Cetonia p. *Fabricius.*

Species. Gymnetis Cærulea: glaberrima, glauca, elytris chalybæis, punctato striatis, maculis albis. Long. Corp. lin $5\frac{1}{2}$.

Gymnetis: very smooth, glaucous, with the elytra chalybeous, striato punctate, and spotted with white. Length $5\frac{1}{2}$ lines.

Syn. Scarabæus cæruleus, *Herbst. in Fuessly Archiv Ins.* 4, *p.* 19, *No.* 8, *t.* 19, *f.* 30. *Gmel. Syst. Nat.* 1582, *No.* 382. *Oliv. Ent.* 1. 6, *p.* 47, *t.* 5, *f.* 31, *a.*
Cetonia 14-maculata, *Fab. Syst. Eleuth.* 2, *p.* 156.

Habitat. India, (*Olivier*). Bengal, (*Donovan*).

The original specimen of Cetonia 14-maculata, described by Fabricius, is now in the collection of the Rev. T. W. Hope, an examination of which has convinced me

1. *Buprestis sternicornis.* 2. *Buprestis chrysis.*

3. *B. confusa.* 4. *B. 4-maculata*

that it is identical with the insect here represented. There are two oblique white spots at the base of the suture of the elytra, which gives the insect the appearance of possessing a distinct scutellum. Olivier, however, correctly described the thorax as being posteriorly lobed, which is the true character of the genus Gymnetis.

BUPRESTIS (STERNOCERA) STERNICORNIS.

Plate III. fig. 1.

TRIBE. STERNOXI, *Latreille.*

FAMILY. BUPRESTIDÆ, *Leach.*

GENUS. BUPRESTIS, *Linnæus.* (SUBGENUS: Sternocera, *Eschscholtz, Solier.*)

SPECIES. BUPRESTIS STERNICORNIS: inauratus, punctis cinereis impressis; elytris serrato-tridentatis; sterno porrecto conico. Long. Corp. 1½ unc.

BUPRESTIS: shining green, with grey impressed spots; elytra serrated, and tridentate at the tips; sternum porrected and conical. Length of the body 1½ inch.

SYN. Buprestis sternicornis, *Linn. Syst. Nat.* I. II. *p.* 610. *Fabricius Ent. Syst.* I. II. *p.* 194. *Oliv. Ent.* II. 32. *p.* 35. *t.* 6. *f.* 52 *a.* *Herbst. Col.* IX. *p.* 16. 2 *t.* 138. *f.* 3.

Among the insects of China is a beautiful species of the genus Buprestis, which the natives of that country collect in considerable numbers, and employ in the various ornaments of their dresses, arms, &c. The Buprestis sternicornis, and chrysis, are collected in India for similar purposes, but being scarce, are esteemed more valuable than the other kind, which they receive at a low price from China.

Both species are brought from Madras and Bombay, but generally in a mutilated state; for the Indians perforate them at both ends, and string them like beads, when they collect them.

BUPRESTIS (STERNOCERA) CHRYSIS.

Plate III. fig. 2.

SPECIES. BUPRESTIS CHRYSIS: thorace viridi; elytris serrato-tridentatis, castaneis lævibus; sterno conico porrecto. Long. Corp. unc. 1½.

BUPRESTIS: with the thorax shining green; the elytra chesnut-coloured, smooth, and terminated by three teeth; sternum conical and porrected. Length 1½ inch.

Syn. Buprestis chrysis, *Fabricius Ent. Syst.* 1. 11. *p.* 194. *Oliv. Ent.* II. 32, *t.* 2, *f.* 8, *a, d, e.* *Herbst. Col.* IX. *p.* 14, 1 *t.* 138, *f.* 2.
Buprestis sternicornis, *De Geer Ins.* IV. *p.* 136. 2, *t.* 17. *f.* 25.

This and the preceding species are alike distinguished by the comparatively small size of the male sex, in which the fifth ventral segment is truncated at its extremity, whereas in the females it is rounded.

BUPRESTIS (SPHENOPTERA?) CONFUSA.

Plate III. fig. 3.

Species. Buprestis Confusa: corpore æneo immaculato, obscure nitido; elytris striatis et tridentatis. Long. Corp. lin. 6.
Buprestis: brassy coloured, without spots, obscurely shining, with the elytra striated and tridentate at the tips. Length ½ inch.

Syn. Buprestis confusa, *Westwood.*
Buprestis ænea, *Fabricius Ent. Syst.* 1. 11. *p.* 193. (*nec ænea, Linnæi.*) *Syst. Eleuth.* 2. *p.* 193. *Donov.* 1*st edit.*
Buprestis tricuspidata, *Oliv. Ent.* 11. 32. *p.* 29. *t.* 8. *f.* 87. *Herbst. Col.* IX. *p.* 181. *t.* 154. *f.* 1. *a, b?*

The original specimen described by Fabricius, was brought from Coromandel by Sir J. Banks. The name applied to it by the former having been previously given by Linnæus to another species, from the south of Europe, (Buprestis, Diceræa, ænea,) it has become necessary to substitute another in its stead, as it is evident that it is not identical with the Buprestis tricuspidata of Olivier, which, according to Schonherr, is from Sierra Leone.

BUPRESTIS (ANTHAXIA) 4-MACULATA.

Plate III. fig. 4.

Species. Buprestis 4-Maculata: elytris integris, viridis; thorace posticé late elytrisque maculis duabus magnis aureis. Long. Corp. lin. 4½.
Buprestis: with the elytra entire; green; hinder part of the thorax with a broad golden band; elytra with two large golden spots on each. Length 4½ lines.

PL. IV

2

1. *Anthia 6_guttata* 2. *Brachinus 2. maculatus*

Syn. Buprestis 4-maculata, *Fabr. Sp. Ins.* I. *p.* 280. *Syst. Eleuth.* 2. *p.* 208. *Olivier Ent.* II. *p.* 32. *t.* 10. *f.* 110. *Herbst. Col.* IX. *t.* 153, *f.* 4.

This admirably beautiful species is described by Fabricius as an inhabitant of India, on the authority of the cabinet of the late Dr. Fothergill. It bears very great resemblance to several brilliant species found in South America and the West Indies, composing the subgenus Actenodes of Dejean. Schonherr, most probably by mistake, has given Italy as the locality of this species.

ANTHIA 6-GUTTATA.

Plate IV. fig. 1.

Tribe. Geodephaga, *MacLeay.*

Family. Carabidæ.

Genus. Anthia, *Weber.*

Species. Anthia 6-Guttata: atra; elytris lævibus; thorace maculis duabus coleoptrisque quatuor albo tomentosis. Long. Corp. 17—21 lin.

Anthia: black, with smooth elytra; thorax with two, and elytra with four white downy spots. Length of the body 17 to 21 lines.

Syn. Carabus sex-guttatus, *Thunberg nov. Sp.* 3. 70. *fig.* 84. *Gmel. Syst. Nat.* 1965. *Fabr. Ent. Syst.* 1. 141. 75. *Syst. Eleuth.* 1. *p.* 221. (Anthia 6-guttata.)

Carabus sex-maculatus, *Donov. edit.* 1. (*nec Fabr. Ent. Syst.* 1. 141. 78. *Syst. Eleuth.* 1. 222.

This conspicuous insect is one of the largest species of the Linnæan genus Carabus. It is very abundant in some parts of India. Donovan, although referring to the original description of A. sex-guttata, published this under the name of Carabus 6-maculatus, which name had been given by Fabricius to a different species of the same genus.

BRACHINUS BIMACULATUS.

Plate IV. fig. 2.

Genus. Brachinus, *Weber.* Carabus p. *Linnæus, Fabricius.*

Species. Brachinus Bimaculatus: capite flavescente; vertice obscuro; thorace obscuro, maculis duabus flavescentibus; elytris nigris, puncto humerali, fascia lata media sinuata abbreviata, apice, antennis pedibusque flavescentibus. Long. Corp. lin. 7—8.

BRACHINUS: with the head yellow; the crown dark coloured; the thorax dark, with two large yellow spots; the elytra black, with a humeral spot; a broad central fascia, interrupted in the middle, and the tips; as well as the antennæ and legs, yellowish. Length 7 to 8 lines.

SYN. Brachinus bimaculatus, *Dej. Spec. gen.* 1. *p.* 299. *Oliv.* III. 35. *p.* 65. *No.* 81. *t.* 2. *fig. a, b, c.* *Schonherr Syn. Ins.* 1. *p.* 229. *No.* 1. (G. Pheropsophus, *Solier.*)

I have not cited Fabricius, nor the other old authorities, as it is evident from their descriptions that they confound several distinct, but nearly allied, species together. Donovan's figure agrees, however, with Dejean's Brachinus bimaculatus, which is from the East Indies.

PLATYRHOPALUS DENTICORNIS.

Plate V. fig. 1.

TRIBE. XYLOPHAGA?

FAMILY. PAUSSIDÆ, *Westwood.*

GENUS. PLATYRHOPALUS, *Westwood.* Paussus p. *Donovan.*

SPECIES. PLATYRHOPALUS DENTICORNIS: brunneo-rufescens; elytris dorso fuscis; suturâ latè ad basin maculâque utrinque posticè, rufescentibus; antennarum clavâ magnâ latere omni acuto, juxta basin externe incisâ. Long. Corp. lin. 4—5.

PLATYRHOPALUS: brownish-red, with the middle of the elytra brown; a broad mark at the base of the suture, and two spots near the extremity red; the club of the antennæ large, ovate, margin acute, with a deep notch near the base behind. Length 4 to 5 lines.

SYN. Platyrhopalus denticornis, *Westwood in Trans. Linn. Soc. vol.* XVI. *p.* 657.
Paussus denticornis, *Donovan,* 1*st edit.*

HABITAT. Bengal.

The first account of the genus Paussus appears in a small tract written by Linnæus, and published at Upsal, in the year 1775, under the title of *Bigæ Insectorum,* &c. This paper contains likewise a description of the Diopsis genus, which, together with the Paussus, are unquestionably two of the most singular genera of the many tribes of insects hitherto discovered. Both may possibly derive some additional celebrity also, from the recollection that the dissertation in which they are inserted, concluded the Entomological labours of that distinguished naturalist: it was the last he ever published in the department of zoology.

PL. V

1 *Platyrhopalus denticornis.* 2 *Paussus thoracicus.*
3 *P. Fichtelii* 4 *P. pilicornis*

COLEOPTERA.

In the dissertation alluded to, the genus Paussus is exemplified by a single species, P. microcephalus, and Diopsis by D. ichneumonea, a plate with figures of both of which, drawn by J. Afzelius, and engraved by Berquist, accompany the descriptions. It is to this plate, and the original descriptions of Linnæus, that Fuessly is indebted solely for the account he gives of both these genera, in his *Archiv. der Insectengeschichte*, printed at Zurich in 1783, as well as in the French translation of that work which afterwards appeared in Paris. Indeed, as Professor Afzelius has suggested, from the repeated errors that appear in those works, in translating the Linnæan observations, defining the character of the genus Paussus, &c., it is very likely that neither Fuessly, nor his translators, Herbst, Gmelin, and some other writers who have treated on it, ever saw an insect either of this genus, or of Diopsis.

Thunberg, during his travels through the country of the Hottentots in 1772, found two coleopterous insects, which he conceived, with much propriety, ought to be referred to a new genus, none of those established previous to his departure from Europe by Linnæus being calculated to admit them. But on his return to Sweden, he found that Linnæus in his absence had described the genus Paussus, to which they might be referred. An account of these was afterwards inserted in the Transactions of the Royal Academy of Stockholm for 1781: this paper is accompanied with a figure of only one of the insects mentioned, P. lineatus, a species very aptly named, from the distinct longitudinal streak on each of the wing cases; the other insect described by Thunberg, he calls ruber. Fabricius consigned these, with the Linnæan insect, to his genus Cerocoma.

The latest history of the genus Paussus, previous to the first edition of this work, was from the pen of Professor Afzelius, a learned, copious, and elaborate paper, inserted in the fourth volume of the Transactions of the Linnæan Society, in which he describes Paussus microcephalus, and another species which he found in Africa, which he names P. sphærocerus. Neither of those insects are allied to the species figured in this plate, which were entirely undescribed. For this important accession of new species to a group so little known, Donovan was indebted to the active and praise-worthy zeal of Mr. Fichtel, in compliment to whom one of them is named Fichtelii.

Since the publication of the first edition of this work, various additional species have been discovered, constituting a very natural family, distributed into several distinct genera, of which I have published a monograph in the sixteenth volume of the Linnæan Transactions. I have also more recently become acquainted with several other species, of which figures and descriptions have been laid before the Entomological Society of London.

Donovan, in order to admit this species into the genus Paussus, was induced to adopt the Linnæan generic character, with the omission of the term "clava solida," although, according to the characters laid down by Afzelius, it ought not to be admitted into the genus, since he states that the tarsi are only three-jointed, whereas in the other species they are five-jointed. They are however four-jointed, but in consequence of the more important variation in the structure of the mouth, which Donovan neglected to examine, I considered it requisite to establish this species as a distinct genus.

PAUSSUS THORACICUS.

Plate V. fig. 2.

GENUS. PAUSSUS, *Linnæus*. Pausus, *Donovan*.

SPECIES. PAUSSUS THORACICUS: ferrugineo-testaceus; elytris disco lateribusque fuscis: antennarum clava oblongâ compressâ trigonâ; latere interno acuto, externo excavato; cavitate ovali marginibus denticulatis. Long. Corp. lin. $3\frac{1}{3}$.

PAUSSUS: pale reddish; the elytra having the disc and sides brown; the club of the antennæ oblong, compressed, and triangular; the inner margin acute, the exterior excavated, with an oval cavity, the margins being denticulated. Length $3\frac{1}{3}$ lines.

SYN. Paussus thoracicus, *Westwood in Trans. Linn. Soc. vol.* XVI. *p.* 640, *pl.* 33, *f.* 28—30.
Pausus thoracicus, *Donovan Ins. Ind.* 1*st edit.*
Paussus trigonicornis, *Latr. Gen. Cr. &c.* 3. *p.* 3, *pl.* 11, *f.* 8. *Sch. Syn. Ins.* 1. *p.* 3, *pl.* 9.

HABITAT. Bengal.

The thorax in this insect is so deeply divided across the middle, that it appears, at first sight, as if it were really two, whence the specific name thoracicus. The same character also exists in P. Fichtelii, which Donovan considered might possibly be the other sex of P. thoracicus; the most striking difference prevailing in the structure of the antennæ, the excavation in one of which is of an oval, or rather shuttle shape, and in the other pyriform. In my monograph I have pointed out other characters, which have induced me to consider the two species as entirely distinct.

COLEOPTERA.

PAUSSUS FICHTELII.

Plate V. fig. 3.

SPECIES. PAUSSUS FICHTELII: testaceus; elytris fuscis, lateribus basi apiceque testaceis; thorace subbipartito; antennarum clavâ oblongâ, latere interno acuto, externo excavato, cavitate pyriformi, marginibus denticulatis. Long. Corp. lin. $2\frac{1}{2}$.

PAUSSUS: pale reddish, with brown elytra, having the sides, base and tips reddish; thorax nearly divided into two parts; club of the antennæ oblong, with the inner margin acute, the external excavated with a pear-shaped cavity, the margins being denticulated. Length $2\frac{1}{2}$ lines.

SYN. Paussus Fichtelii, *Westwood in Trans. Linn. Soc. vol.* XVI. *p.* 641, *pl.* 33, *f.* 31—33.
Pausus Fichtelii, *Donovan Ins. Ind.* 1*st edit.*

HABITAT. Bengal.

There is a specimen of this species in the collection of the Entomological Society of London, presented by the Rev. W. Kirby.

PAUSSUS PILICORNIS.

Plate V. fig. 4.

SPECIES. PAUSSUS PILICORNIS: testaceus; elytris piceis: thorace bipartito; antennarum clavâ oblongâ, apice attenuatâ incurvâ, pilis longis sparsis. Long. Corp. lin. 2.

PAUSSUS: reddish, with pitchy elytra; the thorax nearly divided into two parts; club of the antennæ oblong, attenuated, and incurved at the tip, with long hairs. Length 2 lines.

SYN. Paussus pilicornis, *Westwood in Trans. Linn. Soc. vol.* XVI. *p.* 643.
Pausus pilicornis, *Donovan Ins. Ind.* 1*st edit.*

HABITAT. Bengal.

In the formation of the club composing the second or exterior joint of the antennæ, this species differs altogether from the others: the club is entire or not excavated, and is slightly beset with hairs. Of this species Mr. Fichtel met with only a solitary specimen, as was likewise the case with Paussus Fichtelii.

PREPODES REGALIS.

Plate VI. fig. 1.

TRIBE. RHYNCOPHORA, *Latreille.*

FAMILY. CURCULIONIDÆ, *Leach.*

DIVISION. BRACHYDERIDES, *Schonherr.*

GENUS. PREPODES, *Schonherr.* Circulio, *Linn. &c.*

SPECIES. PREPODES REGALIS: oblongo ellipticus, niger, squamulis cœruleo-virentibus tectus, rostro subcarinato; thorace supra impresso vitta media lateribusque cupreo-aureis; elytris subtilius remote punctato-striatis, plagâ baseos, fasciisque tribus flexuosis cupreo-aureis nigro-marginatis ornatis. Long. Corp. lin. 8.

PREPODES: oblong-elliptical, black, clothed with greenish blue scales; the thorax with a central streak, and the sides golden coppery; the elytra with a basal spot and three waved bands, coppery golden coloured, margined with black. Length 8 lines.

SYN. Curculio regalis, *Linn. Syst. Nat.* I. II. *p.* 616. *Fabr. Syst. Eleuth.* 2. 508. *Oliv. Ent.* V. 83, *t.* 1. *f.* 8, *a*, *b*.

Prepodes (Callizonus, *Olim.*) regalis, *Sch. Sp. Curcul.* 2. *p.* 21.

Donovan well observed that this species truly deserves the title regalis, being an aggregate of beauty and splendour: of the loveliest cœrulean, changing alternately to the deeper glow of the violet, to green, or the transitory sparkling of intermingled silver. Every space of blue is constantly contrasted with another of crimson, and which as the violet changes to blue or green, alters its aspect to a still more vivid expanse of gold. Each of those colours, the blue and red, are distinct; for an irregular space of black limits every spot and marking, and relieves the whole. As the effect of such a combination of colours in this comparatively small species is inconceivably splendid, and almost inimitable, one figure in the plate is intended to show the natural size, and to admit of more perfect delineation, another somewhat magnified is added also.

This insect, which Donovan believed to be *unique* in Great Britain, was brought from France, in the collection of Mons. De Calone, and was in the possession of the author. Linnæus met with it in one of the cabinets on the continent, and described it as a South American insect. In the works of Fabricius, its habitat is given "in *Indiis.*" On this authority Donovan introduced it amongst the insects of *East* India, but it was the practice of Fabricius, and the older authors, to employ the term "in Indiis," to designate the *West* as well as the *East* Indies. The real locality of this species is South America, Peru, and the island of Saint Domingo.

PL. VI

1. Prepodes Regalis. 2. Calandra Palmarum

PL. VII

1. *Fulgora pyrorhina* 2. *Aphana pictura* 3. *Pseudaphana hyalinata*

COLEOPTERA.

CALANDRA PALMARUM.

Plate VI. fig. 2.

Division. Rhyncophorides, *Schonherr.*

Genus. Calandra, *Fabricius.* Rhyncophorus, *Herbst.* Curculio p. *Linn.*

Species. Calandra Palmarum: depressa, atra, obscura; thorace supra plano; elytris abbreviatis striatis; rostro apice compresso, supra piloso. Long. Corp. $1\frac{5}{8}$ unc.

Calandra: depressed, black, not shining; thorax flat above; elytra abbreviated and striated; rostrum compressed at the tip, and hairy above. Length $1\frac{5}{8}$ inch.

Syn. Curculio palmarum, *Linn. Syst. Nat.* 1. 11. *p.* 606. 1. *Fabricius Syst. Eleuth.* 2. 430. *De Geer Ins.* 5. *t.* 15, *f.* 26.

Donovan observes, upon this insect,—" A very abundant species in India, where it is found chiefly on the palm tree." The real locality of this species is South America. De Geer, and Madame Merian giving Surinam; Dejean, Cayenne; and Latreille, South America, Cayenne, and Surinam. The mistake appears to have originated, either by confusing several allied species together, or by giving the West Indies under the name of India generally, as noticed under the last species.

Order. HEMIPTERA, *Linnæus.*

FULGORA PYRORHINA.

Plate VII. fig. 1.

Suborder. Homoptera, *Latreille.*

Family. Fulgoridæ, *Leach.*

Genus. Fugora, *Linnæus.*

Species. Fulgora Pyrorhina: "fronte rostrata adscendente, apice rubra; hemelytris fuscis fascia pallidiori; alis nigris, basi viridibus." *Donovan.* Expans. alar. unc. 4.

Fulgora: with the trunk rostrated, ascending; red at the tip; wing-cases brown, pale across the middle; wings black, green at the base. Expanse of the wings 4 inches.

Syn. Fulgora pyrorhina, *Westwood Mon. Fulgorained.*
Fulgora pyrorhynchus, *Donovan,* 1*st edit.*

" Amongst the more valuable acquisitions, designed to enrich this illustration, few can afford higher gratification to the scientific reader than this Fulgora. In size it is inferior only to F. lanternaria; it is an undoubted nondescript, and may be considered as a striking example of the entomological riches of a country hitherto scarcely known, the interior of Indostan. It was originally brought from India by the late Governor Holford, and is now in the possession of the author. He has sought in vain for this species in other cabinets of exotic insects, and ventures to deem his specimen unique."

Donovan, adopting the opinion of the luminosity of the Fulgoræ, then proceeds:—" In the course of our remarks on the Fulgora so abundant in China, F. candelaria, our attention was naturally directed to the astonishing property some insects of this genus are known to possess, that of emanating light; and it was to this insect we alluded in particular, when speaking of one from interior India, that enabled us to extend our observations on that property. The trunk is large, of a dark purple, thickly sprinkled with spots of white phosphoric powder, and the apex, which is scarlet, and somewhat pellucid, still retains a reddish glow, that almost convinces us the creature when living could diffuse light both from the apex and the spots. In admitting this conjecture, without wandering into the marvellous, its nocturnal appearance must be infinitely more singular than either of the known species of Fulgoræ, Lampyrides, or any other luminous insect yet discovered; for, when on the wing, the illuminated apex would resemble a globule of fire, or heated iron, and the numberless phosphoric spots on the tube, form a train of glittering stars to accompany it.*

" The only figure of a Fulgora in any respect resembling this species, is given in the works of Stoll, under the title of *De Groote Groene Coromandelische Lantaarndrager*;† but among other evident specific distinctions we need only notice the structure of the trunk, which is altogether different, being much recurved, and tapering gradually from the base to an acute point at the apex: its colour is also an olive black."

* " As it may be thought improbable that any insect can exhibit such an extraordinary appearance, the words of Olivier on some species of Lampyrides may not be unsatisfactory. The insects are certainly very distinct, but reports of travellers countenance an opinion that the phosphoric emanations are analogous in the species of both genera. ' The phenomena produced by a natural phosphorous is still more wonderful in some foreign species, in which the males shine, and being provided with wings, will produce in their rapid flight a thousand small stars.'—*Olivier, Histoire des Insectes.*"

† " Pl. 26, fig. 143. Green lantern-carrier fly of Coromandel.—At the conclusion of the description, Stoll says, '*In de Nederlandsche Kabinetten, &c. &c.*'—' This insect was not known in the cabinets of the low countries till within three years, [anno 1780,] during which time a few were brought from Tranquebar, on the Coromandel coast, to the cabinet of natural curiosities of his Highness the Stadtholder of the United Provinces, of which I have been obligingly permitted to take the figure of a female by Mons. Vosmar, to whom I owe my public acknowledgments for it.'—99. *tab.* 26."

HEMIPTERA.

APHANA? FESTIVA.

Plate VII. fig. 2.

GENUS. APHANA? *Burmeister*. Aphæna, *Guerin*.

SPECIES. APHANA? FESTIVA: fronte conica; hemelytris fuscis margine antice virescente punctis 5 atris, quatuor postici inter puncto fulvo; alis sanguineis apice fuscis. Long. (alis clausis) $\frac{4}{5}$ unc.

APHANA? with the trunk short, conical; wing-cases brown, with the front margin greenish, in which are five black spots, the four exterior ones having a fulvous dot; wings sanguineous, with the tips brown. Length with the wings closed $\frac{4}{5}$ of an inch.

SYN. Fulgora festiva, *Fabricius Ent. Syst.* 4. *p.* 5. *Syst. Rhyng, p.* 4.

HABITAT, "Coromandel, *Mus. Dom. Banks*," *Fabricius*.

In addition to the Banksian specimens, still preserved at the Linnæan Society, there is a specimen of this curious species in the collection of the Entomological Society of London, from the Kirbian cabinet. The antennæ being mutilated, I am unable to decide whether it be strictly an Aphana, to which genus, however, it is most nearly allied.

PSEUDAPHANA HYALINATA.

Plate VII. fig. 3.

GENUS. PSEUDAPHANA, *Burmeister*. Dictyophora, *Germar*. Fulgora p. *Fabr*.

SPECIES. PSEUDAPHANA HYALINATA: fronte conica inæquale; hemelytris hyalinis nervis albo nigroque punctatis striaque transversa in medio atra; alis hyalinis, macula apicis atra. Long. alis cl. unc. 1.

PSEUDAPHANA: with the trunk short, conical, uneven above; wing-covers hyaline, with the veins spotted alternately with black and white, and with a transverse black central band; wings hyaline with a black apical spot. Length with the wings shut, 1 inch.

SYN. Fulgora hyalinata, *Fabr. Ent. Syst.* 4. *p.* 5. *Syst. Rhyng. p.* 4.
Pseudaphana h., *Burmeister Handb. der Ent.* 2. *p.* 160. *Germar in Thon's Arch.* 2. *p.* 47.

Fabricius refers to the collection of Sir Joseph Banks, Bart. for this and the preceding species. The annexed figures are copied from the specimens that author has described.—F. Hyalinata is from Bengal.

FULGORA LINEATA.

Plate VIII. fig. 1.

SPECIES. FULGORA LINEATA: fronte rostrata lineari adscendente; hemelytris pallidis, lineis duabus fuscis. Long. alis clausis. unc. ½.

FULGORA: with the trunk linear ascending; hemelytra pale, with two brown longitudinal lines. Length with the wings closed, ½ an inch.

"A pretty little undescribed species, found in Bengal, where it is not very uncommon."—*Donovan.*

An apparent variety of this species is figured in *Griffith's Animal Kingdom,—Insects, pl.* 90, *fig.* 2, from India, under the name of Fulgora pallida, a name which, at all events, must be rejected, having been previously given to the following species.

PSEUDAPHANA PALLIDA.

Plate VIII. fig. 2.

SPECIES. PSEUDAPHANA PALLIDA: "fronte rostrata lineari, adscendente; thorace pallide viridi, rubro lineato; hemelytris hyalinis."—*Donovan.* Long. alis clausis, ½ unc.

PSEUDAPHANA: with the trunk linear, ascending; thorax pale green with red lineations; wing-cases hyaline. Length with the wings closed, ½ an inch.

SYN. Fulgora pallida, *Donovan,* 1*st edit.*

HABITAT. "From the same place as the preceding insect."—*Donovan.*

The small species of Pseudaphana, which is well distinguished from Fulgora by the less closely reticulated wings, are somewhat numerous. Three species have been described as inhabitants of the East Indies, namely Fulgora grammea, *Fabricius (Syst. Rhyng. p.* 4, *"India Orientali.")*; Flata lyrata, *Germar, (Thon's Ent. Archiv.* 2. *p.* 47, *"Bengalia.")*; and Flata splendens, *Germar (Thon's Ent. Archiv.* 2. *p.* 47, *"Java.")*. It is not improbable that Donovan's species may be identical with one of these, possibly the F. lyrata, which is also from Bengal; but from the too concise description of Donovan, which I have copied entire above, it is not possible to speak with absolute precision.

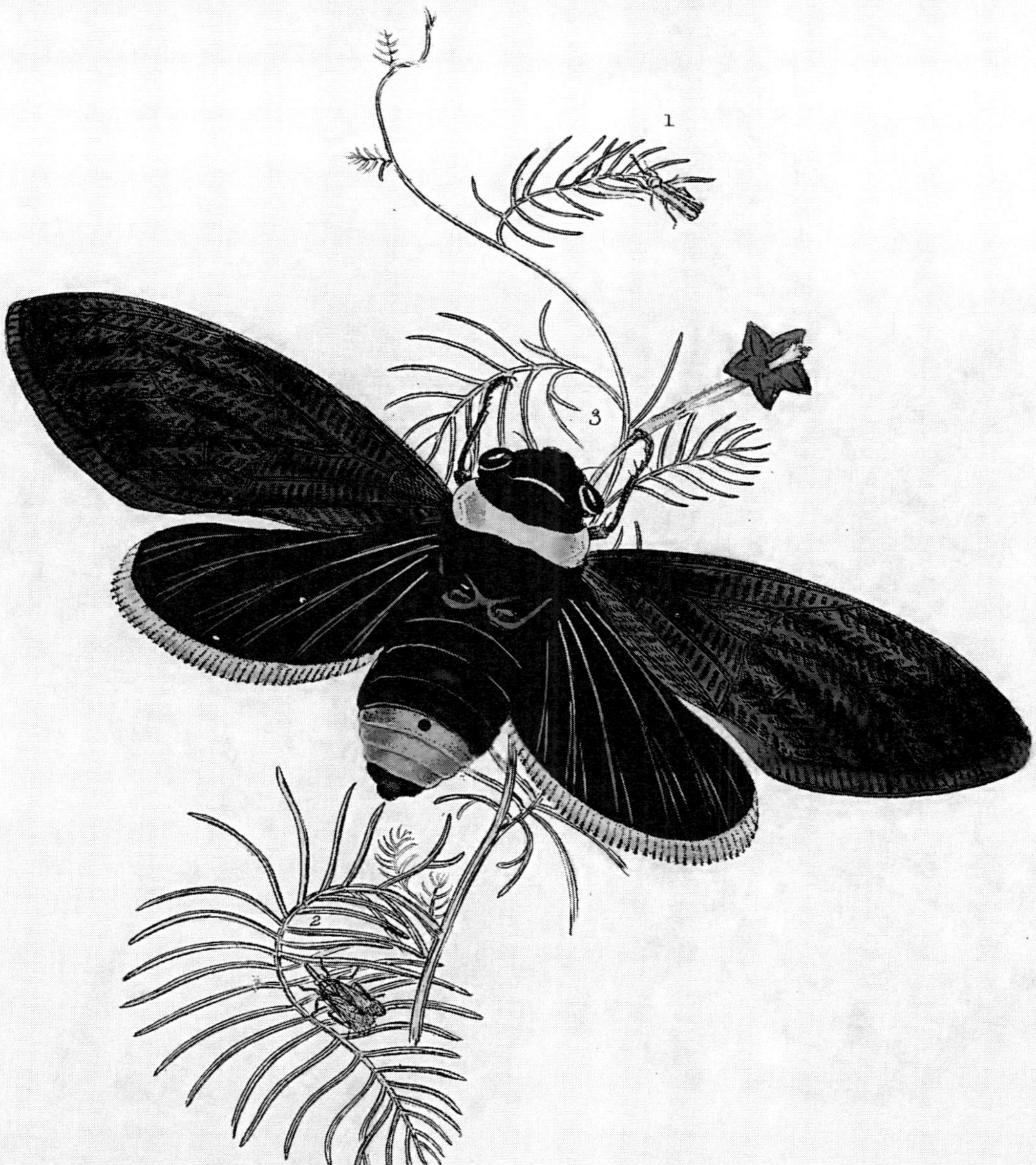

1. Fulgora lineata. 2. Pseudaphana pallida.
3 Cicada speciosa

PL. 1

Phasma Gigas.

CICADA SPECIOSA.

Plate VIII. fig. 3.

Family. Cicadidæ, *Leach.*

Genus. Cicada, *Linnæus.* Tettigonia, *Fabricius.*

Species. Cicada Speciosa : nigra ; thorace fascia lata flava ; abdomine postice fascia aurantia ; hemelytris fusco-olivaceis venis rubris ; alis margine albo. Expans. alar. unc. $6\frac{1}{4}$.

Cicada : black; thorax with a broad yellow fascia; abdomen with the fifth, sixth and seventh segments fulvous above ; hemelytra brown-olive with red veins ; wings with the margin white. Expanse of the wings, $6\frac{1}{4}$ inches.

Syn. Tettigonia speciosa, *Illiger in Wied. Archiv. fur Zool. and Zoot.* 2. 145. 38. *tab.* 2. (1800). *Fabr. Syst. Rhyng, p.* 33.

Cicada Indica, *Donovan,* 1*st edit.*

"This is unquestionably one of the most striking and magnificent species of Cicada we are acquainted with. A single specimen of this kind was discovered in Bengal by Mr. Fichtel about four years ago. It is now deposited in the Imperial cabinet at Vienna." *(Donovan.)*

The species was also contained in the collection of Hellwig, from which it was described and figured by Illiger, in the work above referred to, in the year 1800, for which reason I have retained the latter name as having the priority.

Order. ORTHOPTERA, *Olivier.* (HEMIPTERA p. *Linnæus.*)

PHASMA (CYPHOCRANA) GIGAS.

Plate IX.

Section. Cursoria, *Latreille.*

Family. Phasmidæ, *Kirby.*

Genus. Phasma, *Fabricius.*

Subgenus. Cyphocrana, *Serville.* Mantis, *Linn. Fabr.* Phasma, *Stoll. Fabr.*

ORTHOPTERA.

Species. Phasma (Cyphocrana) Gigas: viridis; mesothorace scabro; tegminibus ovalibus; alis (area costali viridi,) obscuré fulvis fusco undatis; pedibus spinosis, flavo-viridibus. Long. Corp. unc. 7. Expans. alar. unc. 7.

Phasma (Cyphocrana): green; mesothorax scabrous; wing-covers small oval; wings, (with the costal area green,) dirty fulvous with brown waves; legs spinose, yellowish-green. Length 7 inches. Expanse of the wings 7 inches.

Syn. Mantis Gigas, *Linn. Syst. Nat.* 2. 689. *Fab. Ent. Syst. vol.* 2, *p.* 14. *Ent. Syst. Suppl. p.* 187. *Shaw Miscell. pl.* 43. *Donovan,* 1*st edit.* (*nec* Phasma (Diapherodes) Gigas, *Drury,* 2. *pl.* 50.)

Cyphocrana Gigas, *Serville Ann. Sc. Nat.* XXII. *p.* 60. *Gray Synops. Phasm. p.* 35. *Le Geant. Stoll Spectres. pl.* 2, *fig.* 5.

Donovan observed of this insect, that it was the largest species of this very extraordinary genus known, and that this specimen was from the island of Amboyna, where it was rare. It is, however, exceeded in size by the Phasma (Diura) Titan of MacLeay, figured by Gray, in his beautiful Memoir of the Phasmidæ of New Holland, plate 4.

PHASMA (PLATYCRANA) EDULE ♀.

Plate X.

Subgenus. Platycrana, *Gray.* Cyphocrana, *Serville.*

Species. Phasma (Platycrana) Edule: viridis; mesothorace tereti; ♂ scabro, ♀ glabro; tegminibus area costali viridi, basi coccineis; pedibus brevibus, submuticis; femoribus posticis spinosis. Long. Corp. ♀ unc. 6. Expans. alar. unc. 4½.

Phasma (Platycrana): green; with the mesothorax slender; scabrous in the male, smooth in the female; wing-covers with the costal area green, pink at the base; legs short, almost smooth; posterior femora spined. Length of the body ♀ 6 inches. Expanse of the wings 4½ inches.

Syn. Phasma edule, *Licht. in Linn. Trans. tom.* 6, *p.* 13.

Mantis viridis, *Donovan,* 1*st edit.*

Le Spectre verd, *Stoll, pl.* 6, *fig.* 20 ♀, 21 ♂.

Mantis viridana, *Oliv. Enc. Meth.* 7. 636. *Serville Revis. Orthopt. p.* 33. (*Ann. Sc. Nat.* 20. *p.* 60.) *Gray Synops. Phasm. p* 36. (Platycrana v.)

Donovan states that he received this species also from Amboyna, where it is, perhaps, more scarce than the preceding insect.

Pl

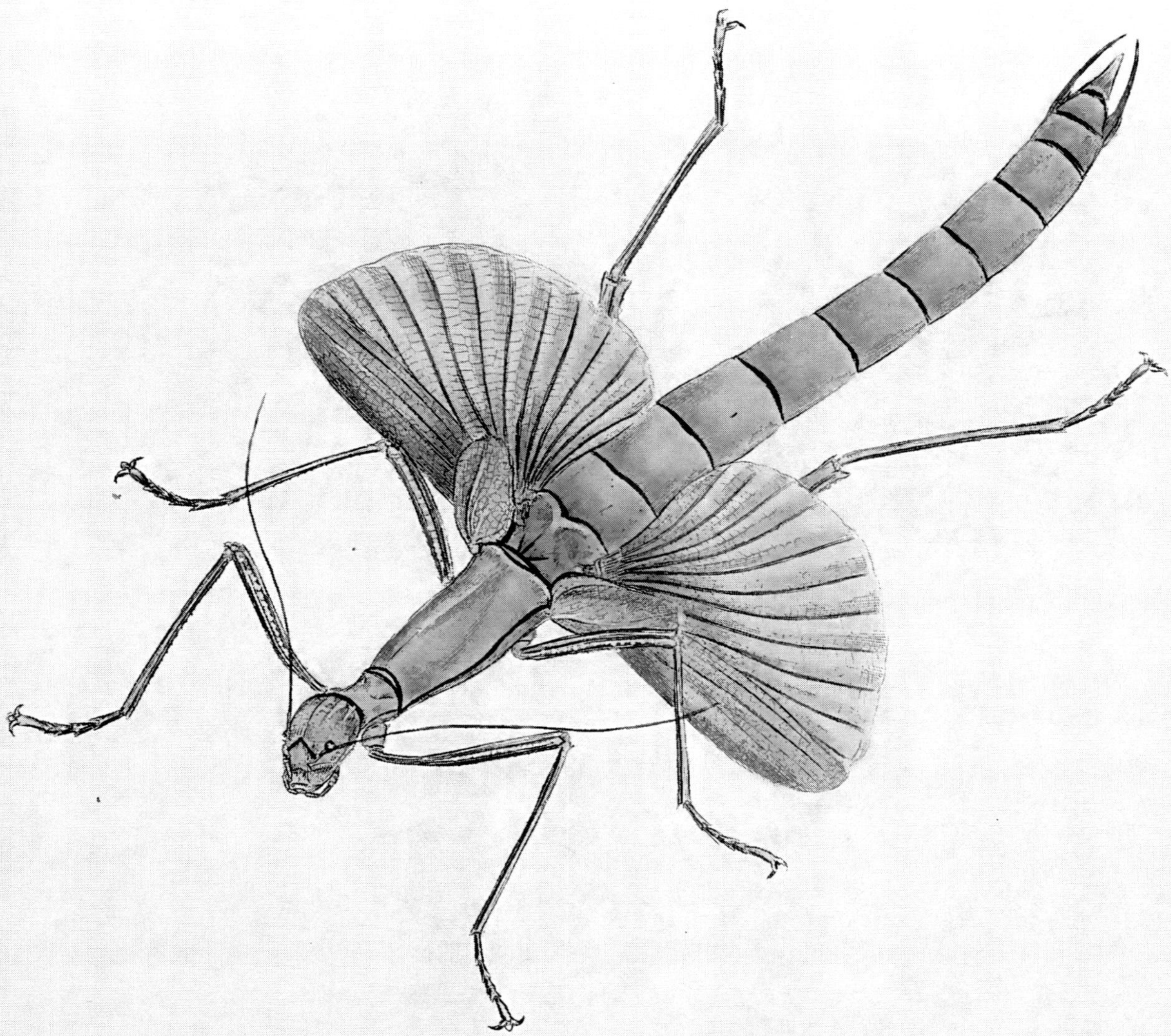

Phasma Edule

PL. XI

1. 2. Phyllium siccifolium. 3. Ph. Donovani (Pupa)

ORTHOPTERA.

PHYLLIUM SICCIFOLIUM.

Plate XI. fig. 1. (Pupa, fig. 2.)

GENUS. PHYLLIUM, *Illiger*, *Latr.* Mantis, *Fabr. Donovan.* Pteropus, *Thunberg.*

SPECIES. PHYLLIUM SICCIFOLIUM: viride; capite, thorace, pedibusque luteo-viridibus; femoribus ovatis membranaceis; tibiis quatuor posticis inermibus; thorace denticulato. Long. Corp. 3½ unc.

PHYLLIUM: green; with the head, thorax, and legs tinged with luteous; the femora ovate, membranaceous; the four posterior tibiæ not dilated; thorax toothed at the sides. Length of the body, 3½ inches.

SYN. Mantis siccifolia, *Linn. Mus. Lud. Reg.* III. *Syst. Nat.* 2. *p.* 689. *Fabr. Ent. Syst.* 2. *p.* 18. *Donovan, 1st edition.*

La Feuille de citron, *Stoll. Spectr. pl.* 7, ♂, ♀, *larva et pupa* (antennis ♀ et pupæ? vitiosis.)

Phasma citrifolium, *Lichtenstein Trans. Soc. Linn. t.* 6, *p.* 17.

Phyllium (1) brevicorne, *Latr. Gen.* 3. *p.* 39, ♀. (Phyllium, *sect.* 11, ♂ *ibid.*)

Phyllium siccifolium, *Lat. R. An.* (2*d edit.*) 5. 179. (*Edit. Crochard*) *Ins. Livr.* I. *pl.* 79, *fig.* 1. (*with details, fig.* 16, *pupa maris nec imago* ♂). *Serville Revis. Orthopt. p.* 36. (*Ann. Sc. Nat.* 22. 63.) *Gray Synopsis Phasm. p.* 30.

"An erroneous opinion has prevailed pretty generally among naturalists respecting the colour of this insect, which when living they conceived to be similar to that of a dried or withered leaf. This, it may be observed, is commonly the appearance of the insect after death: such was no doubt the colour of the specimens delineated by Roesel; nor can we for a moment hesitate in believing that the insects described by the accurate Linnæus and Dr. Shaw exhibited the like appearance. The specimen of the winged insect in our cabinet, has been preserved, however, with more than usual care. Immediately after the death of the creature, as we have reason to suspect, the abdomen had been opened, and so nicely excavated that no portion of the entrails, or oily fluids, which would have inevitably destroyed the true colour, was allowed to remain. The natural colour is therefore preserved, which is not of a pale brown, as is commonly imagined, but of a delicate, lovely green; a colour dependant, it appears, upon a thin internal coating immediately beneath the outer skin, the latter of which is perfectly transparent, and destitute of any colour.

"The pupa of this curious species is represented, together with the perfect insect, on the Vinca rosea.

"There is also a much smaller pupa depicted in the upper part of the plate, that was discovered in one of the islands of the Indian seas, and belonged to the celebrated

Mr. Bailey, the astronomer who sailed in one of the expeditions with Captain Cook. This is of an analogous kind to that of the Mantis siccifolia, though evidently distinct. The perfect insect, and in consequence the species, is unknown to us. Our only motive for inserting it is to shew the peculiar singularity of the abdomen, in the middle of which there are two remarkable subquadrangular spots, of a filmy texture, that are transparent, and may be seen through very distinctly."—*Donovan.*

Mr. G. R. Gray, in his *Synopsis of the Phasmidæ*, has characterized the last named insect as a distinct species, with the description:—

P. Donovani (Pupa): viride, abdomine medio maculis duabus hyalinis subquadratis. Long. Corp. 1—5. Exp. Corp. 6¾.

The chief character of this supposed insect is, I believe, indicative only of the males, notwithstanding the shortness of the antennæ in the accompanying figure, which it is not improbable are fictitious, the antennæ of the male pupæ being much longer, and more numerously articulated, than in the females. If this supposition should be ascertained to be correct, I have little doubt that the figure in question represents merely the male pupa of Ph. siccifolium, and not of a distinct insect. In the Crochard edition of the *Regne Animal*, a figure is given of the male pupa, which is described as the perfect state of that sex; but unfortunately only the three basal segments of the abdomen are represented, the fourth, which bears the ocelli, and the remaining segments being omitted.

LOCUSTA (MONACHIDIA) RETICULATA.

Plate XII. fig. 1.

SECTION. SALTATORIA, *Latreille.*

FAMILY. LOCUSTIDÆ, *Leach.*

GENUS. LOCUSTA.

SUBGENUS. MONACHIDIA. (Monachidium, *Serville.*)

SPECIES. LOCUSTA (MONACHIDIA) RETICULATA: ferruginea; thorace crista trifida carinata, postice producta cymbiformi, carina lineaque laterali nigris; tegminibus nigris flavo reticulatis. Long. (alis clausis) unc. 2½.

LOCUSTA (MONACHIDIA): ferrugineous; thorax with a three-cleft, keeled, boat-shaped crest produced over the elytra, the ridge and a lateral line of black; tegmina black, reticulated with yellow. Length with the wings shut, 2½ inches.

SYN. Gryllus reticulatus, *Fabr. Ent. Syst.* 11. *p.* 47. *Donov.* 1*st edit.*

Fabricius describes this insect from the Banksian collection, and as an inhabitant of Tranquebar.

Pl. X.

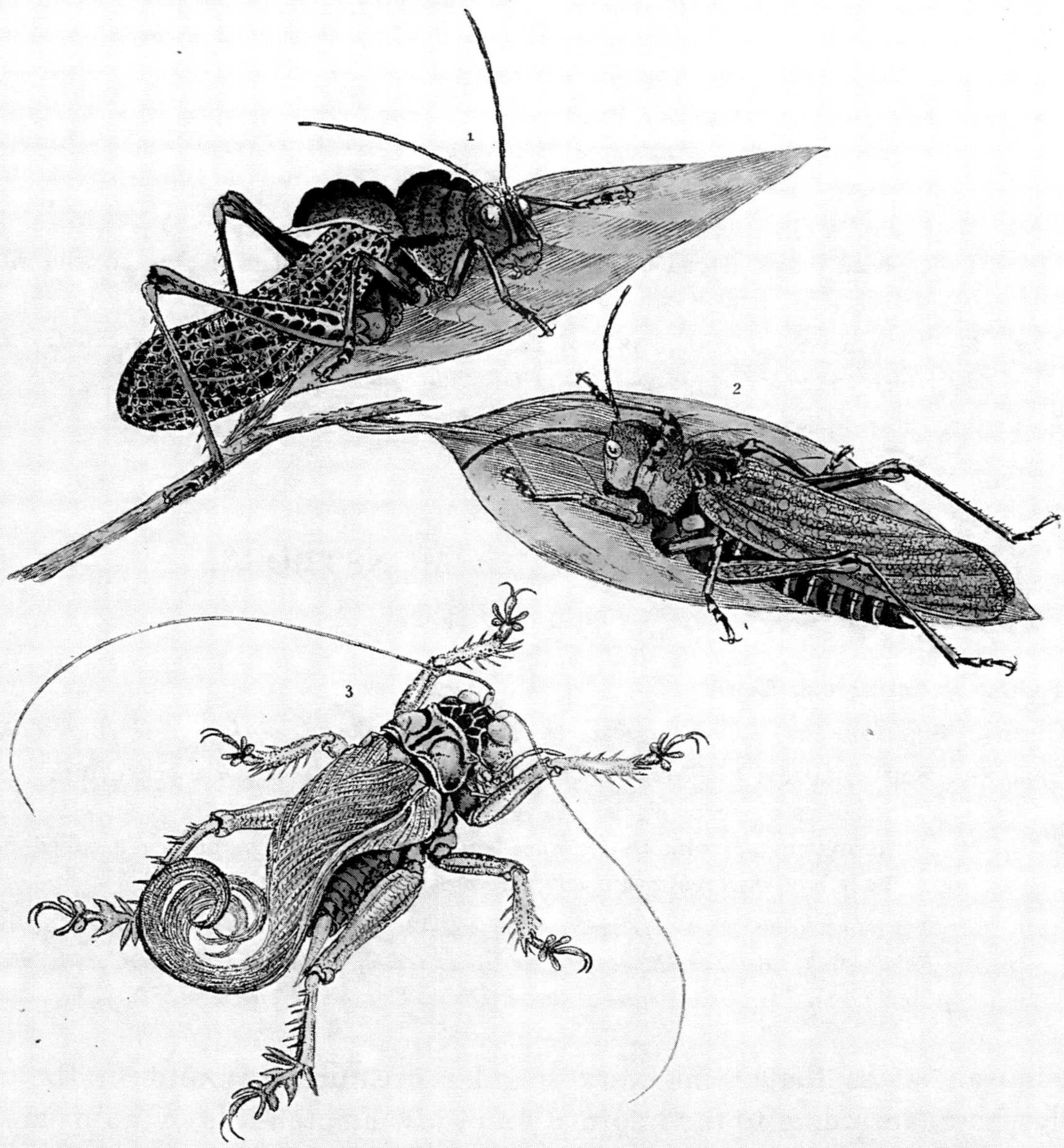

3. *Schizodactyla monstrosa.* 1. *Locusta reticulata.*

2. *Locusta punctata.*

ORTHOPTERA.

LOCUSTA (PHYMATEA) PUNCTATA.

Plate XII. fig. 2.

SUBGENUS. PHYMATEA. (Phymateus, *Thunberg, Serville.*)

SPECIES. LOCUSTA (PHYMATEA) PUNCTATA: thorace verrucoso atro, lateribus capitis et thoracis flavis; tegminibus atris, flavo-punctatis; alis atris; abdomine rufo-annulato. Long. (alis clausis) 2¾ unc.

LOCUSTA (PHYMATEA): with the thorax warty, black, with the sides of it and of the head yellow; tegmina black, spotted with yellow; wings black; abdomen with red rings. Length, (with the wings shut,) 2¾ inches.

SYN. Gryllus punctatus, *Drury, App. vol.* 2, *pl.* 41, *fig.* 4. *Fabr. Ent. Syst.* 2. 51. *Thunberg, Mem. Acad. Petersb. p.* 258. *Stoll Saut. pl.* 7 *b, f.* 24 *A.*

HABITAT. East Indies.

SCHIZODACTYLA MONSTROSA.

Plate XII. fig. 3.

FAMILY. ACHETIDÆ, *Leach.*

GENUS. SCHIZODACTYLA. (Schizodactylus, *Brulle.* Acheta, *Fabricius.* Gryllus, *Latreille.*

SPECIES. SCHIZODACTYLA MONSTROSA: tegminibus alisque caudatis convolutis; corpore luteo-fusco punctis nigris. Long. Corp. 1⅝ unc.

SCHIZODACTYLA: with the tegmina and wings very long, forming a rolled-up-tail; body luteo-fuscous with black markings. Length 1¾ inches.

SYN. Gryllus monstrosus, *Drury App. vol.* 2, *pl.* 43, *fig.* 1. *Fabricius Ent. Syst.* 2. 29. (Acheta m.) *Aud. et Brulle Hist. Nat. Ins. t.* 9, *p.* 161.] *British Cycl. Nat. Hist. pl. of Orth. Ins. Le Regne Animal (Edit. Crochard,) Ins. pl.* 82, *f.* 1.

Donovan states that "this very singular creature is found in the vicinity of Bengal, where, according to the information of Mr. Fichtel, it is by no means common. It lives under ground, like the Gryllus Campestris, and some other well known analogous European insects of this tribe."

This fact is of considerable interest, since it clearly proves the strong relation which exists between this interesting species and the family of the crickets, Achetidæ; a relation strengthened, moreover, by the general structure of the body; the anal appendages, (one of which is shewn in the accompanying figure); the horizontal position of the dorsal part, and the vertical position of the lateral part of the tegmina; as well as the general colour of the insect.

M. Brullé has very judiciously formed this insect into a new group, which he has named Schizodactylus, from the remarkable structure of the tarsi, which are furnished with curious dilated plates, and are four-jointed. It is chiefly on this account M. Brullé has removed this insect to the family of the grasshoppers, with long antennæ, (Gryllidæ, *Leach.* Locustaires, *Latr.*). M. Brullé has also been induced to adopt this arrangement, by the greater length of the maxillary palpi, and the large size of the wings. The last mentioned character is, however, especially that of many of the crickets, (Achetidæ,) for instance, the common house cricket; and the size of the palpi is scarcely a character of first-rate importance. M. Brullé has moreover omitted to notice, that the anterior tibiæ are destitute of that peculiar oval cavity which he expressly states (p. 125) to be found "dans *tous* les insects de cette famille." Hence, from the majority of its characters, I am still induced to place this insect in the family Achetidæ, regarding it as the connecting link between that family and the Gryllidæ. The genus Anostostoma of Gray, (*Mag. Nat. Hist. 2nd series,* 1. *p.* 143.) is another very interesting link.

PHYLLOPHORA AMBOINENSIS.

Plate XIII. fig. 1.

FAMILY. GRYLLIDÆ, *Leach.* Locustaires, *Latreille.*

GENUS. PHYLLOPHORA, *Thunberg.* Steirodon, *Serville.* Locusta p. *Fabricius.*

SPECIES. PHYLLOPHORA AMBOINENSIS: "viridissima; thorace tetragona, ângulis dentatis; scutello [sc. area interna tegminum] magno fusco-viridi; elytris foliaceis latissimis."—*Donovan.* Long. alis clausis, unc. 4½.

PHYLLOPHORA: green; thorax quadrangular, with the angles dentated; scutel large, brown-green; wing-cases leaf-formed and very broad. Length, with the wings closed. 4½ inches.

SYN. Locusta Amboinensis. *Donov.* 1*st edit.*

"The only specimen we have ever seen of this elegant species, is that delineated in the annexed plate with Locusta citrifolia. This insect was received from Amboyna some years ago by Governor Holford, then resident in India, and is at this time in the collection of the author.

PL. XIII

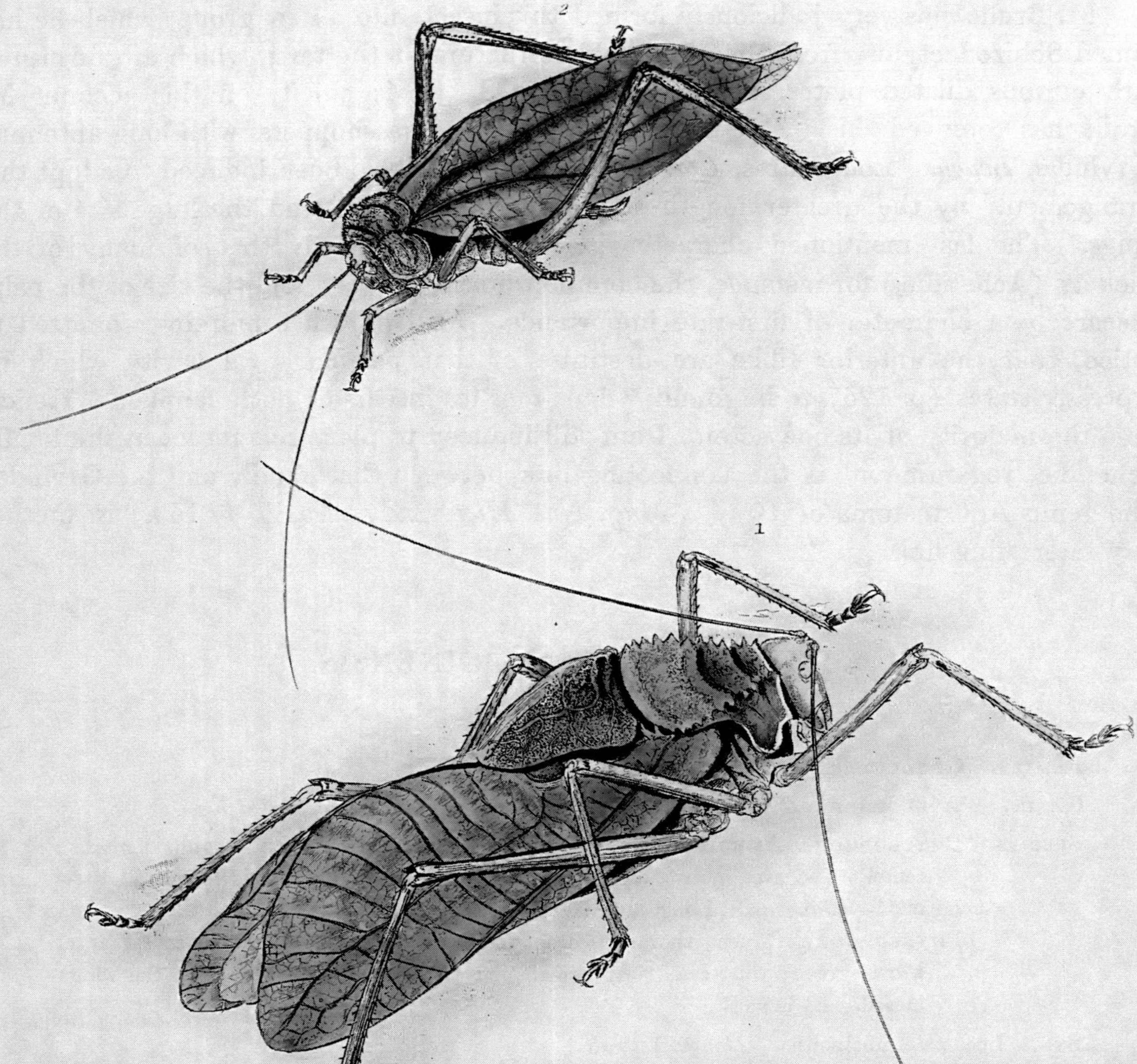

1. *Phyllophora Amboinensis.* 2. *Ph. citrifolia.*

"Both the elytra, or wing-cases, and the posterior part of the thorax, are of a fine delicate green; the anterior part of the thorax yellowish brown; with the head and body still paler. The wing-cases, as usual in this tribe, bear no very distant resemblance to the leaves of certain plants, not only in colour, but also in the outline, and still more so in the conformation of the nerves which arise and branch off towards the extremities, exactly in the same manner as the nerves arise, and ramify, from the midrib in the leaves of the far greater number of plants. One peculiarity in the structure of the elytra in our new species deserves remark: the scutel, or rather that portion of the wing-case on the left side that folds over the back when the creature is at rest, is of a much stronger texture than any other part of the insect, except the thorax, and serves as an external covering or defence to the corresponding lobe of the other wing-case, which is of a more delicate nature, consisting only of a thin and pellucid membrane, the surface of which is hyaline or glassy. The wings are remarkably tender, of a whitish colour, and semitransparent."—*Donovan.*

PHYLLOPHORA CITRIFOLIA.

Plate XIII. fig. 2.

SPECIES. PHYLLOPHORA CITRIFOLIA: thorace tetragono, angulis crenatis; tegminibus viridibus, folium lauri referentibus. Long. alis clausis, unc. 3.

PHYLLOPHORA: with the thorax quadrangular, crenated at the angles; wing-covers green like a laurel leaf. Length, with the wings closed, 3 inches.

SYN. Gryllus citrifolius, *Linnæus, Mus. Reg. Ulr. p.* 125. *Syst. Nat.* II. 695. *Fabricius, Ent. Syst. t.* 2. *p.* 33, (Locusta c.) *De Geer Mem. vol.* 3, *pl.* 33, *f.* 3. *Serville, Rev. Orth. p.* 44. Steirodon c.)

HABITAT. "In Indiis," (*Linnæus.*) Surinam, (*De Geer.*) Cayenne, (*Serville.*)

Donovan states that he received it with the preceding insect from Amboyna.

Order. HEMIPTERA, *Linnæus.* (continued.)

RAPHIGASTER INCARNATUS.

Plate XIV. fig. 1.

SECTION. HETEROPTERA, *Latreille.*

FAMILY. PENTATOMIDÆ, *Leach.* Cimex, *Linn.*

GENUS. RAPHIGASTER, *Laporte.*

SPECIES. RAPHIGASTER INCARNATUS: supra sanguineus; capite, scutelli maculis duabus; hemelytris unica, membranaque apicali nigris. Long. Corp. unc. 1.

RAPHIGASTER: above sanguineous, with the head; two spots on the scutellum; a single one on each of the hemelytra, and the apical membrane black. Length 1 inch.

SYN. Cimex incarnatus, *Drury Illustrations, App. vol.* 2, 1*st edit. pl.* 36, *f.* 5.
Cimex nigripes, *Fabr. Syst. Rhyng.* 149. 17. *Wolff,* 1, *t.* 2, *f.* 11. *Donovan* 1*st edit.*
Cimex melanopus, *Gmel. Syst. Nat.* 2149.

This beautiful species bears a distant similitude to Cimex aurantius, described among the insects of China; it is found in the environs of Batavia, as we are informed, but is by no means common there.

TESSERATOMA PAPILLOSA.

Plate XIV. fig. 2.

GENUS. TESSERATOMA, *St. Farg. et Serv. Laporte. Burmeister.*

SPECIES. TESSERATOMA PAPILLOSA: lutea; thoracis lateribus subrotundatis; antennis fuscis, basi subferrugineis; abdomine supra purpureo-ferruginono. Long. Corp. unc. 1.

TESSERATOMA: luteous; thorax with the sides rounded; antennæ dark brown, reddish towards the base; abdomen above purplish-ferruginous. Length 1 inch.

SYN. Cimex papillosus, *Drury, App. vol.* 2, *pl.* 43, *f.* 2. *(nec Fabr. Burmeister, &c.) Donovan,* 1*st edit.*
Tesseratoma Sonneratii, *St. Farg. et Serv. Enc. Méth.* 10. 590.
Cimex Chinensis, *Thunberg, Nov. Ins. t.* 11, *f.* 59. *Laporte, Hemipt. p.* 60.

" Professor Thunberg describes this Cimex under the name of Chinensis. Our figures represent both the larva and the perfect insect. That our specimens are from the East Indies need not admit of doubt: the same kind is mentioned as a native of Sierra Leone by Fabricius, perhaps without sufficient authority."—*Donovan.*

There is, perhaps, some doubt, as to this species being the C. Chinensis of Thunberg, or the real papillosus of Drury. The African species, described by Fabricius under the latter name, is totally distinct. See my observations on this insect, in the second edition of *Drury's Illustrations, vol.* 2, *p.* 91.

PENTATOMA CRUCIATA.

Plate XIV. fig. 3.

GENUS. PENTATOMA, *Latreille.* Cimex, *Fabricius. Burm.*

SPECIES. PENTATOMA CRUCIATA: nigro pallidoque varia; scutello nigro, cruce alba. Long. Corp. unc. $\frac{1}{3}$.

PENTATOMA: pale yellow with black spots, (10 on the thorax, 4 in front, and 6 behind); scutellum black, with a white cross. Length $\frac{1}{3}$ of an inch.

SYN. Cimex cruciata, *Fabr. Ent. Syst.* 4. 119. *Syst. Rhyng. p.* 174. *Wolff Cimic. t.* 7, *f.* 59.

Fabricius states that this species was found in the East Indies by Dr. Kœnig. Donovan's specimen was from Bengal.

PENTATOMA MACTANS.

Plate XIV. fig. 4.

SPECIES. PENTATOMA MACTANS: ovata depressa; supra rufa, thorace scutelloque maculis duabus; hemelytrorumque membrana apicali nigris. Long. Corp. $\frac{1}{2}$ unc.

PENTATOMA: ovate depressed; above rufous, with two black spots on the thorax, and two on the scutellum; apical membrane of the hemelytra black. Length $\frac{1}{2}$ inch.

SYN. Lygæus Mactans, *Fabr. Ent. Syst.* 4. 161. *Syst. Rhyng. p.* 227.
Cimex Mactans, *Fabr. Sp. Ins.* 2. 366. *Donovan,* 1*st edit.*

ACANTHOSOMA UNIGUTTATA.

Plate XIV. fig. 5.

GENUS. ACANTHOSOMA, *Curtis.* Cimex, *Donovan.*

SPECIES. ACANTHOSOMA UNIGUTTATA: thorace acute spinoso; ferruginea, scutello puncto magno albo notato. Long. Corp. unc. $\frac{1}{2}$.

HEMIPTERA.

Acanthosoma: with the thorax produced on each side into an acute spine; ferruginous, with a large white spot at the base of the scutellum. Length $\frac{1}{2}$ an inch.

Syn. Cimex uniguttatus, *Donovan, 1st edit.*

Donovan states that this curious species is a native of Madras.

RHYNCHOCORIS VIRIDIS.

Plate XIV. fig. 6.

Genus. Rhynchocoris, *Westwood.* Cimex, *Donovan.*

Species. Rhynchocoris Viridis: thorace spinoso; viridis; hemelytris fusco-cinereis; scutello apice flavescenti; thoracis spinis cylindricis truncatis. Long. Corp. unc. $\frac{4}{5}$.

Rhychocoris: with the thorax produced behind on each side into a cylindric spine, truncate at the tip; green; hemelytra brownish-grey; scutel at the tip yellowish. Length $\frac{4}{5}$th of an inch.

Syn. Cimex viridis, *Donovan, 1st edit.*

This rare insect is from Ceylon.

RHYNCHOCORIS HAMATA.

Plate XIV. fig. 7.

Species. Rhynchocoris Hamata: thorace acute spinoso, testacea; elytris virescentibus; abdomine serrato; denticulis nigris. Long. $\frac{9}{10}$ unc.

Rhynchocoris: with the thorax produced into an acute spine on each side, testaceous buff, with greenish elytra; the margin of the abdomen serrated; the teeth black. Length $\frac{9}{10}$th of an inch.

Syn. Edessa hamata, *Fabr. Ent. Syst.* 4. 104. *Syst. Rh. p.* 147.
Cimex serratus, *Donovan, 1st edit.*
Rhynchocoris hamata, *Westwood, in Cat. Hemipt. Mus. Hope.*

Java, and other parts of the East Indies.

PL. XIV.

1. Raphigaster incarnatus. 2. Tesseratoma papillosa. 3. Pentatoma cruciata. 4. P. mactans. 5. Acanthosoma uniguttata. 6. Rhynchocores viridis. 7. Rh. hamata.

Pl. X

1. Papilio Antenor. 2 Papilio Antiphus.

Order. LEPIDOPTERA, *Linnæus.*

PAPILIO ANTENOR.

Plate XV. fig. 1.

TRIBE. DIURNA, *Latreille.* GENUS: Papilio, *Linn.*, (Butterflies.)

FAMILY. PAPILIONIDÆ, *Leach.*

GENUS. PAPILIO, *Latreille.* (Papiliones Equites, *Linn.*)

SPECIES. PAPILIO ANTENOR: alis dentatis concoloribus atris albo-maculatis; posticis caudatis; disco atomis viridibus lunulisque marginalibus rubris. Expans. alar. 6 unc. 6 lin.

PAPILIO: with the wings dentate, black with many white spots, the posterior pair tailed, and with the disk powdered with green atoms, the margin with red lunules. Expanse of the wings 6½ inches.

SYN. Papilio Antenor, *Drury, Ill. Exot. Ent. vol.* 2 *app. pl.* 3, *f.* 1, 2*d edit. v.* 2, *p.* 4. *Fabr. Ent. Syst.* III. I. *p.* 4, *No.* 9. *Jablonsky, Pap.* 2. *t.* 3, *fig.* 1. *Boisduval Hist. Nat. Lepid.* 1, *p.* 189. *No.* 2. *Enc. Méth.* 9, 69.

HABITAT. Tropical Africa.

This species was originally described by Drury, from whom all subsequent writers (including Donovan) have derived their descriptions and figures of this exceedingly rare butterfly. Drury states that he was unaware from what country his specimen was obtained. Fabricius, however, gave India as its country, on which authority, apparently, Donovan introduced it into this work, observing that it might "be numbered with much propriety among the rarest of the Papilio tribe found in India." In the second edition of Drury's Illustrations, I have stated the incorrectness of this locality, on the authority of a specimen in the collection of the Rev. F. W. Hope, brought from tropical Africa by the late Mr. Ritchie. Had the insect moreover been an inhabitant of India, it would surely have been received more frequently. No specimen however, as far as I am aware, is contained in any of the continental collections.

PAPILIO ANTIPHUS.

Plate XV. fig. 2.

SPECIES. PAPILIO ANTIPHUS: alis concoloribus nigris, anticis ad apicem griseo radiatis, posticis caudatis, lunulis septem submarginalibus rubris. Expans. alar. 3 unc. 3 lin.

PAPILIO: with all the wings similarly coloured, black; the anterior paler, greyish at the tips, with black rays; the posterior pair tailed, and with seven red lunules. Expanse of the wings $3\frac{1}{4}$ inches.

Syn. Papilio Antiphus, *Fabr. Ent. Syst.* III. 1. *p.* 10. *Enc. Méth.* 9. 71. *Boisduval Hist. Nat. Lepid. vol.* 1, *p.* 266.

Var. Papilio Polygius, *Enc. Méth.* 9. 811.

Habitat: India, (*Fabricius*). Philippine Islands, (*Enc. Méth.*) Manilla, (*Boisduval*).

Nearly allied to Papilio Polydorus, but one-fifth smaller, and without the white spot on the posterior wings. It was originally described by Fabricius from the unpublished collection of drawings of Mr. Jones, from which it is most probable that Donovan, who had access thereto, obtained this figure, which is the only one yet published of the species. In the *Encyclopédie Methodique,* a variety of this species, with nine red lunules, is described under the name of Papilio Polygius, from the Philippine islands, where this insect appears to replace Papilio Polydorus.

ORNITHOPTERUS PRIAMUS.

♂ Plate XVI.

Genus. Ornithopterus. (Ornithoptera, *Boisduval.*)

Species. Ornithopterus Priamus: alis holosericeis supra viridibus, limbo nigro; anticis fascia longitudinali latissima; posticis maculis submarginatibus, nigris; his denticulatis abdomine flavo ♂, Expans. alar. unc. $8\frac{1}{2}$.

Ornithopterus: with the wings silky; above green with a black border, the anterior with a very broad longitudinal black bar, the posterior with black submarginal spots, the latter wings denticulated, the abdomen yellow, ♂. Expanse of the wings $8\frac{1}{2}$ inches.

Syn. Papilio (Equ. Tr.) Priamus, *Linn. Amœn. Acad.* 5. 3. *f.* 203. *Syst. Nat.* 2. 744. *Clerck Icones, t.* 17. *Fabr. Ent. Syst.* III. 1. *p.* 11. *Cramer, pl.* 23, *A. B. Enc. Méth.* 9, *p.* 25. *Boisduval Hist. Nat. Lepid. vol.* 1, *p.* 173.

Donovan observes, that "With the exception of Papilio Ulysses, which perhaps in point of splendour may excel, Papilio Priamus is beyond comparison the most lovely creature of this tribe of insects hitherto discovered, either in India or any other country. It is a native of Amboyna, where we understand it is extremely rare, and bears a considerable price among the Dutch amateurs in that island. We obtained a pair of them in fine condition some years ago from the cabinet of the late Mr. Tunstall, who had purchased them in Holland, from a collection made by one of the Dutch governors in Amboyna. This rarity is figured in a resting position on the blossoms of the Mimosa Grandiflora."

PL. XV.

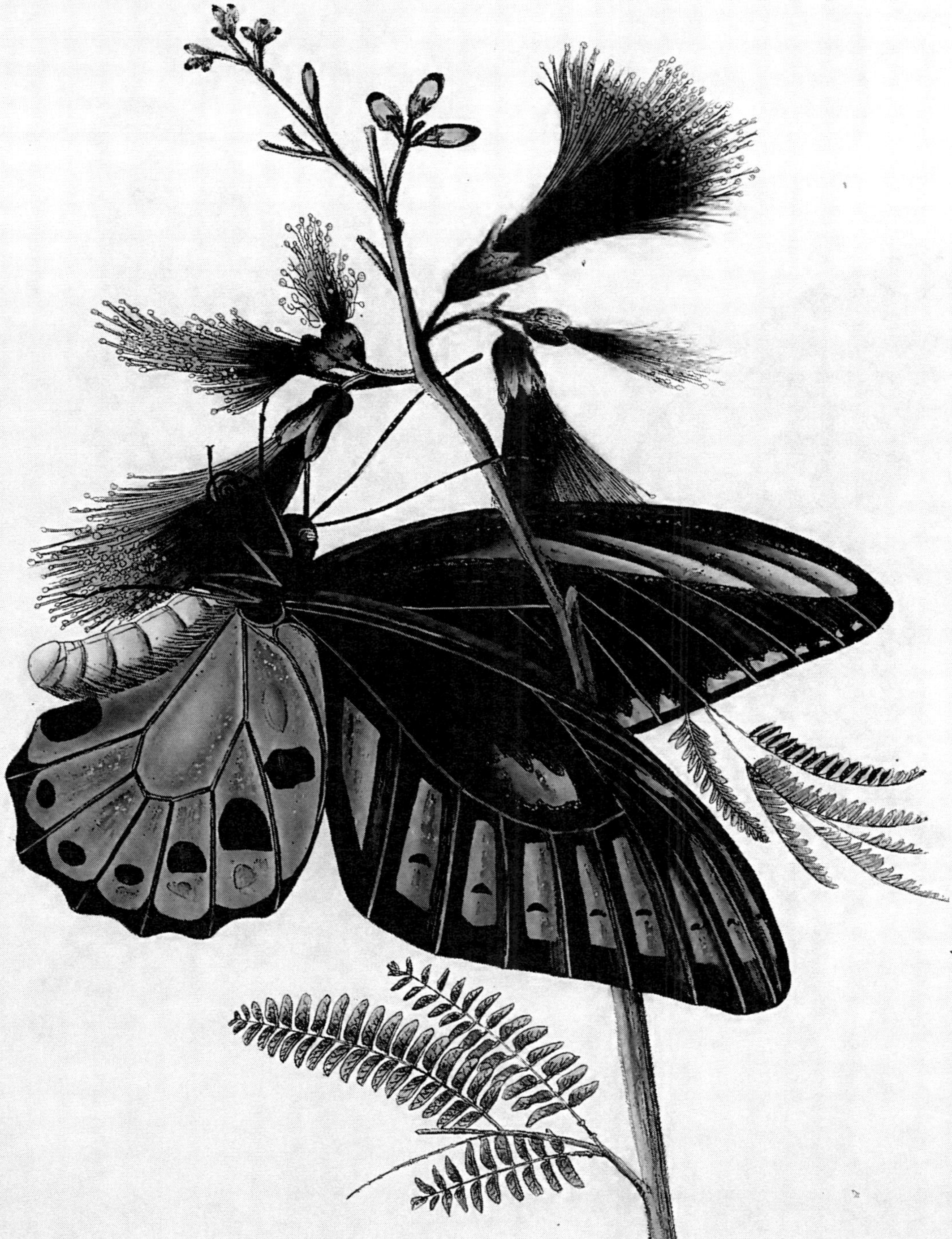

Ornithoptera Priamus

1 Papilio Empedocles. 2 Papilio Deiphobus.
3 Papilio Lacedemon.

LEPIDOPTERA.

PAPILIO EMPEDOCLES.

Plate XVII. fig. 1.

SPECIES. PAPILIO EMPEDOCLES: alis fuscis; anticis utrinque fascia maculari viridi, transversa media, posticis caudatis, subtus ad angulum ani lunulis duabus nigris. Expans. alar. unc. $4\frac{1}{2}$.

PAPILIO: with the wings brown; the anterior on both sides with a transverse central band of green spots; the posterior tailed, and with two black lunules at the anal angle beneath. Expanse of the wings $4\frac{1}{2}$ inches.

SYN. Papilio (Nymphalis) Empedocles, *Fab. Ent. Syst.* III. 1. *p.* 70. *Enc. Méth.* 9. 810. *Boisduval Hist. Nat. Lepid. vol.* 1, *p.* 29.

HABITAT. "India Orientali," (*Fabricius.*) Island of Bourbon, (*Boisduval.*)

The original Fabrician description was taken from a specimen in the collection of Sir Joseph Banks, now in the possession of the Linnæan Society. By Fabricius this species was inserted, by some strange oversight, amongst the Nymphales.

PAPILIO DEIPHOBUS.

♂ Plate XVII. fig. 2.

SPECIES. PAPILIO DEIPHOBUS: alis nigris subtus basi rubro-maculatis; posticis candatis maculis septem rubris subannularibus submarginalibus. ♂. Expans. alar. unc. 6.

PAPILIO: with black wings, the base beneath being spotted with red; the posterior pair tailed, with seven red subannular and submarginal spots. Expanse of the wings 6 inches.

SYN. Papilio (Eq. Tr.) Deiphobus, *Linn. Syst. Nat.* 2. 746. *Clerck Icon. t.* 25. *Cramer, t.* 181, *A. B. Fabricius Ent. Syst.* III. 1. *p.* 5. *Enc. Méth.* 9. 64. *Boisduv. Hist. Nat. Lepid. vol.* 1, *p.* 200.

♀ Papilio Alcandor, *Cramer, pl.* 40, *A. B.*

The female has the wings brown above, the posterior pair being ornamented with a large palmated buff mark in the centre. Boisduval gives the Moluccas, Amboyna, and Celebes, as the habitat of this species.

PAPILIO LACEDEMON.

Plate XVII. fig. 3.

SPECIES. PAPILIO LACEDEMON: alis dentatis nigro-fuscis, lunulis marginalibus albis; posticis ecaudatis subtus brunneis lunulis submarginalibus nigris. Expans. alar. unc. $4\frac{1}{4}$.

PAPILIO: with the wings dentated, brownish-black, with marginal lunules; the posterior without tails, beneath brown, with black submarginal lunules. Expanse of the wings $4\frac{1}{4}$ inches.

SYN. Papilio (Eq. Ach.) Lacedemon, *Fabr. Ent. Syst.* III. 1, *p.* 36. *Boisduval Hist. Nat. Lepid. vol.* 1, *p.* 374. *Enc. Méth.* 9. 38.

HABITAT. Malabar, (*Fabricius*).

ORNITHOPTERUS REMUS.

Plate XVIII.

SPECIES. ORNITHOPTERUS REMUS: alis nigris; posticis dentatis, subtus albis, his utrinque maculis submarginalibus auratis. Expans. alar. unc. $9\frac{1}{2}$.

ORNITHOPTERUS: with black wings; the posterior pair dentate, beneath (except at the base) white, with golden coloured submarginal spots more or less expanded. Expanse of the wings $9\frac{1}{2}$ inches.

SYN. Ornithoptera Remus, *Boisduval Hist. Nat. Lepid. p.* 176, (nec Priamus ♀ *p.* 173).
Papilio Remus, *Fabr. Ent Syst.* III. 1, *p.* 11. *Cramer, pl.* 135 *A,* 136 *A, and* 386 *A. B. Enc. Méth.* 9, *p.* 126. *Naturalist's Lib. Entomol. v.* 5, *pl.* 1, *f.* 2.
Papilio Panthous, *Donovan,* 1*st edit.*

Donovan observes of this species, that "it is one of the many magnificent natural productions of Amboyna, and is extremely rare." By Donovan it was given as the Papilio Panthous, with the further observation, "The supposed female of this insect is also considered as the female of Papilio Priamus; it is a gigantic creature, being still larger than the butterfly represented, but it is less beautiful, and the general colour an obscure reddish brown." The insect here referred to by Donovan is the real Papilio Panthous, and is now generally considered to be the true female of P. Priamus. The insect here figured is evidently a male, as may be seen from the anal valve, which so peculiarly distinguishes the males of the Ornithopteri. Hence Godart and Boisduval must be in error in giving this figure as the female of Priamus. In the nearly uniform colour of the upper wings it better agrees with P. Remus, although the markings of the posterior wings are different. I have not, however, ventured to give it as a distinct

Ornithoptera Remus.

XIX

1 Ornithoptera Heliacon. 2 Papilio Idæus

species, considering it possible that the markings may be liable to variation. It is figured resting on a flower of the double variegated Japan rose, a scarce variety of the Camellia Japonica.

In the Naturalist's Library, Entomology, vol. 5, p. 89, this figure is given as the female of Priamus, although a figure agreeing with the present is likewise given under the name of Remus.

ORNITHOPTERUS HELIACON.

Plate XIX. fig. 1.

SPECIES. ORNITHOPTERUS HELIACON: alis dentatis anticis nigris, posticis flavis limbo tenui undata punctisque submarginalibus nigris. Expans. alar. unc. 5½.

ORNITHOPTERUS: with the wings dentated; the anterior black, the posterior golden yellow, with a festooned black margin, and with a row of black submarginal spots, of which the two exterior are the largest, the others being often obsolete. Expanse of the wings 5½ inches.

SYN. Papilio (Eq. Tr.) Heliacon, *Fabr. Ent. Syst.* III. 1. *p.* 19, 60. *Boisduval Hist. Nat. Lepid. p.* 178. (Ornithoptera H.)
Papilio Amphrisius ♂, *Enc. Méth.* 9, 27. *Horsfield Lep. Jav. pl.* 4, *f.* 3.
Papilio Astinous, *Fab. Ent. Syst.* III. 1. *p.* 19.
Papilio Minos, *Cramer, pl.* 195 *A.*
Papilio Pompeus, *Cramer, pl.* 25 *A.*
Amphrisius Nymphalides, *Swainson Zool. Illustr. new series, pl.* 98.

Originally described by Fabricius from the Banksian Collection and Mr. Jones's drawings; and as the present figure exactly agrees with the Fabrician description, it is most probable that it was from one of these sources (to both of which Donovan had access) that this figure was taken. This is of some importance, as the species has been confounded with several others, as may be seen from the synonyms quoted above, and as it is liable to considerable variation in the spots of the posterior wings, and in the occasional paler radiation of the superior wings. In a specimen which I possess, exactly corresponding with this figure, the neck has a scarlet band, and there are some scarlet bands at the sides of the thorax beneath.

The transformations of this species have been observed by Dr. Horsfield in Java, and figures of the larva and pupa published in the *Lepidoptera Javanica, (pl.* 4, *f.* 13). The caterpillar is thick, of a yellowish colour, with a broad dorsal white line. It is armed with eight rows of erect obtuse fleshy appendages, as well as with a furcate tubercle behind the head. The chrysalis is thick, curved and armed on the back of each of the three intermediate abdominal segments with a pair of conical points.

Dr. Horsfield considers this insect as the type of the last of the three great sections of the genus Papilio having the antennæ with obscure annuli, (vide synopt. table). Mr. Swainson gave it as a subgenus named Amphrisius, confounding the two species Heliacon and Amphrisius together, and applying the latter name as that of the genus. But as Priamus and its allies are the *types* of the same group, it would be absurd, even were it not inconvenient, to retain this genera name. I have therefore employed M. Boisduval's name of Ornithoptera, altering its termination, however, to make it agree with the sex of the old genus Papilio, from which it has been separated.

PAPILIO IDÆUS.

Plate XIX. fig. 2.

SPECIES: PAPILIO IDÆUS: alis nigris, anticis fascia abbreviata flava, posticis dentatis, macula palmata trifida punctisque sanguineis, emarginaturis albidis. Expans. alar. unc. $4\frac{1}{4}$.

PAPILIO: with black wings, the anterior with an abbreviated yellow band, the posterior dentated, with a palmated mark composed of three red united spots, and several other red spots, the emarginations yellowish. Expanse of the wings $4\frac{1}{4}$ inches.

SYN. *Fabricius, Ent. Syst.* III. 1. *p.* 16. *Enc. Méth.* 9. 33. *Boisduval Hist. Nat. Lepid. p.* 299.

HABITAT. Madras, *Fabricius.*

This species was originally described from the collection of Mr. Drury, and Mr. Jones's drawings, which evidently supplied Mr. Donovan with the present figure. The French Entomologists are only acquainted with the species through the works of Fabricius and Donovan. M. Boisduval is of opinion, that from the facies of this species it is rather an inhabitant of South America than the East Indies.

PAPILIO ASTYANAX.

Plate XX. fig. 1.

SPECIES. PAPILIO ASTYANAX: alis nigris concoloribus, anticis fascia sesquialtera alba striata, posticis dentatis, ecaudatis, macula discoidali palmata lunulisque sex submarginalibus sanguineis. Expans. alar. unc. 4.

PAPILIO: with all the wings black, the anterior having a broad oblique whitish band, striped with black beyond the middle, united to another shorter, which crosses the

PL.

2. Papilio Astyanax 1 Papilio Polymnestor

discoidal cell; the posterior wings dentated without tails, with a discoidal palmated blotch, and six submarginal lunules of a sanguineous colour. Expanse of the wings, 4 inches.

Syn. Papilio Astyanax, *Fabricius, Ent. Syst.* III. 1. *p.* 13. *Enc. Méth.* 9. 72. *Boisduval, Hist. Nat. Lepidopt.* 271.

Papilio Mutius, ♀? *Fabr. loc. at p.* 3.

It is most probable that this figure represents an injured individual of Papilio Mutius, which differs only from Astyanax in possessing tails to the posterior wings. This might have occurred through the tails having been broken off, or, as in Papilio Polydorus, some individuals of P. Mutius may possess only very rudimental tails. The species was originally described by Fabricius from the collection of Mr. Drury, and the drawings of Mr. Jones, from which it is probable Mr. Donovan obtained this figure, and from which alone the French Entomologists are acquainted with the species. I possess the late Mr. Haworth's specimens of P. Mutius, which together with the remainder of that gentleman's collection of Papilionidæ, were compared with Mr. Jones's drawings, and which are labelled "P. Astyanax?" the mark of doubt being probably added from the difference in the tail.

The P. Astyanax of the earlier works of Fabricius, is a totally different insect, and a native of America.

PAPILIO POLYMNESTOR.

Plate XX. fig. 2.

Species. Papilio Polymnestor: alis dentatis, nigris; anticis fascia lata transversa submarginali albida, (venis interrupta); posticis apice cærulescenti-plumbeis, maculis atris ordinatim digestis. Expans. alar. unc. 6½.

Papilio: with the wings dentated, black; the anterior having a broad transverse submarginal whitish band, (interrupted by the veins); the posterior wings with the terminal half leaden-blue, with two rows of black spots. Expanse of the wings, 6½ inches.

Syn. Papilio (Eq. Tr.) Polymnestor, *Fab. Ent. Syst.* III. 1. *p.* 18. *Cramer, tab.* 53, *figs. A, B.* Papilio Polymnestor, *Enc. Méth.* 9. 29. *Boisduval, Hist. Nat. Leid. p.* 191.

Habitat. "Various parts of India," (*Donovan*). Cachemere, Ceylon, (*Boisduval*).

PAPILIO ULYSSES.

Plate XXI.

SPECIES. PAPILIO ULYSSES: alis nigris, disco cæruleo radiante, posticis caudatis; subtus ocellis septem. Expans. alar. unc. 5¼.

PAPILIO: with black wings, the disc being blue and radiated, posterior wings tailed; beneath brown, with seven large submarginal ocelli on the posterior wings. Expanse of the wings, 5¼ inches.

SYN. Papilio (Eq. Ach.) Ulysses, *Linn. Syst. Nat.* 2. 748. *Fabr. Ent. Syst.* III. 1. *p.* 23. *Enc. Méth.* 9. 65. *Cramer, tab.* 121, *f. A, B. Boisd. Hist. Nat. Lepid.* 1, *p.* 202.
♀ Papilio Diomedes, *Linn. Syst. Nat.* 2. 749. *Cramer, t.* 122, *fig. A.*

HABITAT. "The Dutch spice islands," (*Donovan*). Amboyna, Celebes, (*Boisduval*).

CASTNIA EVALTHE.

Plate XXII.

SECTION. —— ? (Hesperi sphinges, *Latreille.*)

FAMILY. CASTNIIDÆ, *Westw.*

GENUS. CASTNIA, *Latr. God. Dalman.* Papilio, (Festivi,) *Fabr.*

SPECIES. CASTNIA EVALTHE: alis integris nigris, nitidis; anticis utrinque fasciis duabus, posticis unica flavis; his supra serie e maculis submarginalibus, subtus pagina omni rubris; fascia maculari flava. Expans. alar. 4¼ unc.

CASTNIA: with the wings entire black, shining; the anterior above and beneath with two bands, and the posterior with a single (sometimes interrupted) band of a yellow colour, the latter have also a submarginal row of red spots, the under surface is also red, with a central row of buff spots. Expanse of the wings, 4¼ inches.

SYN. Papilio (Festiv.) Evalthe, *Fab. Ent. Syst.* III. 1. *p.* 45. *Syst. Ent. p.* 480. *Herbst. Pap. t.* 137, *f.* 1, 2. *Enc. Méth.* 9. 797. (Castnia E.) *Donovan,* 1*st edition.* (Papilio E.)
Papilio Dardanus, *Cramer, pl.* 17, *fig. E, F.*

HABITAT. "In Indiis," (*Fabricius*).* Surinam and Brazil, (*Enc. Méth.*)

This scarce and beautiful species, represented on a sprig of the Vitex Negundo, Fine-leaved Chaste tree, is here misplaced, not only on account of its belonging

* By the term "In Indiis," Fabricius meant either the West or the East Indies; although he more generally employed the term "In India," or "In India orientali," to designate the habitats of East Indian species.

Papilio Ulysses

Castnia Evalthe.

PL. XXIII

1. Vanessa Lethe. 2. Nymphalis Coelas.
3. N. (Charaxes) Tiridates.

to the section of the Hesperi-sphinges of Latreille, but also, because it and all the other species of the remarkable genus to which it belongs, are inhabitants of the tropical parts of South America.

VANESSA LETHE.

Plate XXIII. fig. 1.

FAMILY. NYMPHALIDÆ, *Leach.*

GENUS. VANESSA, *Latr. God. Curtis.* Hamadryades, *Hubn.* Papilio (Nymph. Phal. *Fabr.*)

SPECIES. VANESSA LETHE: alis subcaudatis supra fulvis; anticis apice late nigro, fascia maculisque flavis; posticis margine flavo striga nigra. Expans. alar. 2—2½ unc.

VANESSA: with the posterior wings shortly tailed, fulvous above; the anterior wings with the extremity broadly black, in which is an oblique fascia and several spots of a yellowish colour; the posterior wings have the margin yellowish, with several parallel narrow black submarginal lines. Expanse of the wings, 2 to 2½ inches.

SYN. Papilio (Nymph.) Lethe, *Fabr. Ent. Syst.* III. 1, *p.* 80. *Enc. Méth.* 9. 818. (Vanessa L.)

HABITAT. "In Indiis," (*Fabricius*). Brazil, (*Enc. Méth.*)

Like the last species, the term applied by Fabricius to indicate the habitat of this species, evidently led Donovan to give it as an inhabitant of the East Indies. It is, however, according to the *Encyclopédie Méthodique,* as well as its very near ally, Vanessa Zabulina, an inhabitant of Brazil.

NYMPHALIS COCLES.

Plate XXIII. fig. 2.

GENUS. NYMPHALIS, *Latreille.* Papilio (Nymphalis) *Fabricius.* Paphia, *Horsfield.*

SPECIES. NYMPHALIS COCLES: alis albo, fusco, flavescentique strigosis, fascia media communi alba; posticis subcaudatis; subtus albidis striga punctorum ocellatorum. Expans. alar. unc. 2.

NYMPHALIS: with the wings transversely streaked with white, brown and yellowish, and with a narrow white bar running across all the wings beyond the middle; posterior wings with short tails; beneath whitish with a row of eyelets. Expanse of the wings, 2 inches.

Syn. Papilio (N.) Cocles, *Fabr. Ent. Syst.* III. 1, *p.* 65. *Enc. Méth.* 9. 362, (Nymphalis C.)

Habitat. Siam, (*Mus. Banks.*)

This insect, together with P. Periander, figured in plate 37, and some other allied species, constitute a very well marked group in the great genus Nymphalis.

NYMPHALIS (CHARAXES) TIRIDATES.

Plate XXIII. fig. 3.

Genus. Nymphalis. (Subgenus: Charaxes, *Boisduval.* Jasia, *Swainson.*)

Species. Nymphalis (Charaxes) Tiridates: alis supra atro-cæruleis; margine postico lunulis ochraceis; omnium dimidio apicali punctis cærulescentibus. Expans. alar. unc. 4¼.

Nymphalis: with blue-black wings; the posterior margin with ochre-coloured lunules; the apical half of all the wings with cærulescent spots. Expanse of the wings, 4¼ inches.

Syn. Papilio (Nymph.) Tiridates, *Fabr. Sp. Ins.* 2, *p.* 11. *Ent. Syst.* III. 1, *p.* 62. *Cramer, pl.* 162, *f. A, B.* *Herbst. Pap. t.* 62, *f.* 3, 4. *Enc. Méth.* 9. 354. (Nymphalis T.) *Drury Ill. v.* 3, *pl.* 23, *f.* 1, 2.

Habitat. Amboyna, (*Fabricius*). Amboyna and Java, (*Enc. Méth.*). Brazil, (*Drury*, but incorrectly?).

IDEA AGELIA.

Plate XXIV.

Family. Heliconiidæ, *Swainson.*

Genus, Idea, *Fabricius*, (*Syst. Gloss. in Illig. Mag.*) Papilio, (Dan. Cand.) *Linnæus.*

Species. Idea Agelia: alis ovatis integerrimis albo-denudatis, venis maculisque nigris; anticis margine externo nigro serie punctorum alborum. Expans. alar. unc. 6¼.

Idea: with ovate and very entire wings, semi-transparent white, with black veins and spots; the outer margin of the anterior wings being black with a row of white spots. Expanse of the wings, 6¼ inches.

Syn. Idea Agelia, *Enc. Méth.* 9. 195. *Audouin et Brullé Hist. Nat. Ins. Lep. t.* 2, *pl.* 5. Papilio (D. C.) Idea, *Linn. Syst. Nat.* 2. 758. *Fabr. Ent. Syst.* III. 1. *p.* 185. *Clerck Icon. tab.* 38, *f.* 1.

Donovan observes of this insect—“ There is a peculiar delicacy in the appearance of this large and rare Papilio that strongly recommends itself to our attention, and,

PL. XXIV

Idea Agelia

PL. XXV

1. Pieris Hippia. 2. Danais Affinis.
3. Nymphalis Philomela.

notwithstanding that the figure of it has a place already in several works on Entomology, impels us to include it in the present selection of Indian insects. Clerk, Cramer, and Drury, have each given a delineation of it, the latter of whom names it Papilio Lynceus; but it is almost superfluous to add, that it is beyond dispute the Papilio Idea of Linnæus. Our specimens are from Amboyna, and are represented on the common Indian Yellow Jasmine."

Although it is evident that this figure of Donovan's represents the true Linnæan Papilio Idea, that figured by Drury is a distinct species, for which the name of Idea lyncea must be retained. Dr. Horsfield has figured another species, from Java, under the name of Idea Gaura, (*Lep. Jav. pl.* 6, *f.* 1. *Boisduval Lepid. pl.* 11, *f.* 11). A fourth, Idea Daos, is figured by M. Boisduval, in the last named work, (*pl.* 24, *fig.* 3); and I believe a fifth was in the collection of General Hardwick, now at the British Museum.

PIERIS HIPPIA.

Plate XXV. fig. 1.

FAMILY. PAPILIONIDÆ, *Leach.*

GENUS. PIERIS, *Schrank, Latr. God.* Papilio (Dan. Cand.) *Linnæus.*

SPECIES. PIERIS HIPPIA: alis repandis virescenti-albis; venis limboque (albo punctato) nigris. Expans. alar. unc. 3¼.

PIERIS: with broad greenish white wings; the veins and borders black, the latter often with white spots. Expanse of the wings, 3¼ inches.

SYN. Papilio (Festiv.) Hippia, *Fabr. Ent. Syst.* III. 1. *p.* 59. *Enc. Méth.* 9. 19. 3, (Danais H.) Pieris Valeria, *Cramer, pl.* 85, *f. A. Enc. Méth.* 9. 155. *Boisduval Hist. Nat. Lep. p.* 444.

HABITAT. "Poulicandor, *Mus. Banks,*" (*Fabricius*). Java, India, (*Boisduval, Enc. Méth.*)

This species has somewhat the facies of some of the Danai, which probably induced Fabricius to remove it from its legitimate situation.

DANAIS AFFINIS.

Plate XXV. fig. 2.

FAMILY. HELICONIIDÆ, *Swainson.*

GENUS. DANAIS, *Latreille.* Euplæa, *Fabricius.* Papilio (Dan. festiv. p. *Linn.*)

SPECIES. DANAIS AFFINIS: alis nigris albo maculatis; posticis dentatis, subtus limbo fusco punctis flavis albisque ordinatim digestis. Expans. alar. unc. 3¼.

DANAIS: with the wings black, spotted with white; the posterior dentate, and beneath with a broad brown border, with one row of fulvous, and two rows of smaller white spots. Expanse of the wings, $3\frac{1}{4}$ inches.

SYN. Papilio (Fest.) affinis, *Fabr. Ent. Syst.* III. 1. *p.* 58, 181. *Syst. Ent. p.* 511. *Enc. Méth.* 9, 182.

HABITAT. "Nova Hollandia, *Mus. Dom. Banks*," (*Fabricius*).

I know not upon what authority Donovan introduced this species amongst the inhabitants of India, New Holland being the only locality recorded by Fabricius, by whom alone the insect has been described, the French Entomologists merely copying his description.

NYMPHALIS PHILOMELA.

Plate XXV. fig. 3.

SPECIES. NYMPHALIS PHILOMELA: alis nigris, anticis albo punctatis et lineatis; posticis basi flavo-radiatis, apice nigris albo-punctatis. Expans. alar. unc. 3.

NYMPHALIS: with the wings black, the anterior with white spots and lines, the posterior radiated with yellow at the base, with a black border spotted with white. Expanse of the wings 3 inches.

SYN. Papilio (Fest.) Philomela: *Ent. Syst.* III. 1, *p.* 57. *Enc. Méth.* 9. 398, (Nymphalis? Ph.)

HABITAT. "In Indiis, *Mus. Dom. Banks*," (*Fabricius*).

PIERIS (IPHIAS) LEUCIPPE.

Plate XXVI. fig. 1.

GENUS. PIERIS, *Schrank, Latreille, Godart.* Colias, *Horsfield.* (SUBGENUS: Iphias, *Boisduval.*)

SPECIES. PIERIS (IPHIAS) LEUCIPPE: alis anticis supra vivide fulvis, venis margineque nigris; posticis supra flavis, subtus saturatioribus atomis fuscis. Expans. alar. unc. $4\frac{1}{2}$.

PIERIS (IPHIAS): with the anterior wings above rich orange, with black veins and border; the posterior pair above yellow, beneath darker with brown atoms. Expanse of the wings $4\frac{1}{2}$ inches.

SYN. Papilio (Dan. Cand.) Leucippe, *Fabr. Sp. Ins.* 2, *p.* 44. *Ent. Syst.* III. 1, *p.* 198. *Cramer Pap. pl.* 36, *fig. A, C. Herbst. Pap. t.* 109. *Enc. Méth.* 9. 119. (Pieris L.) *Boisduval Hist. Nat. Lepid.* 1. 596. (Iphias L.)

HABITAT. The Island of Amboyna.

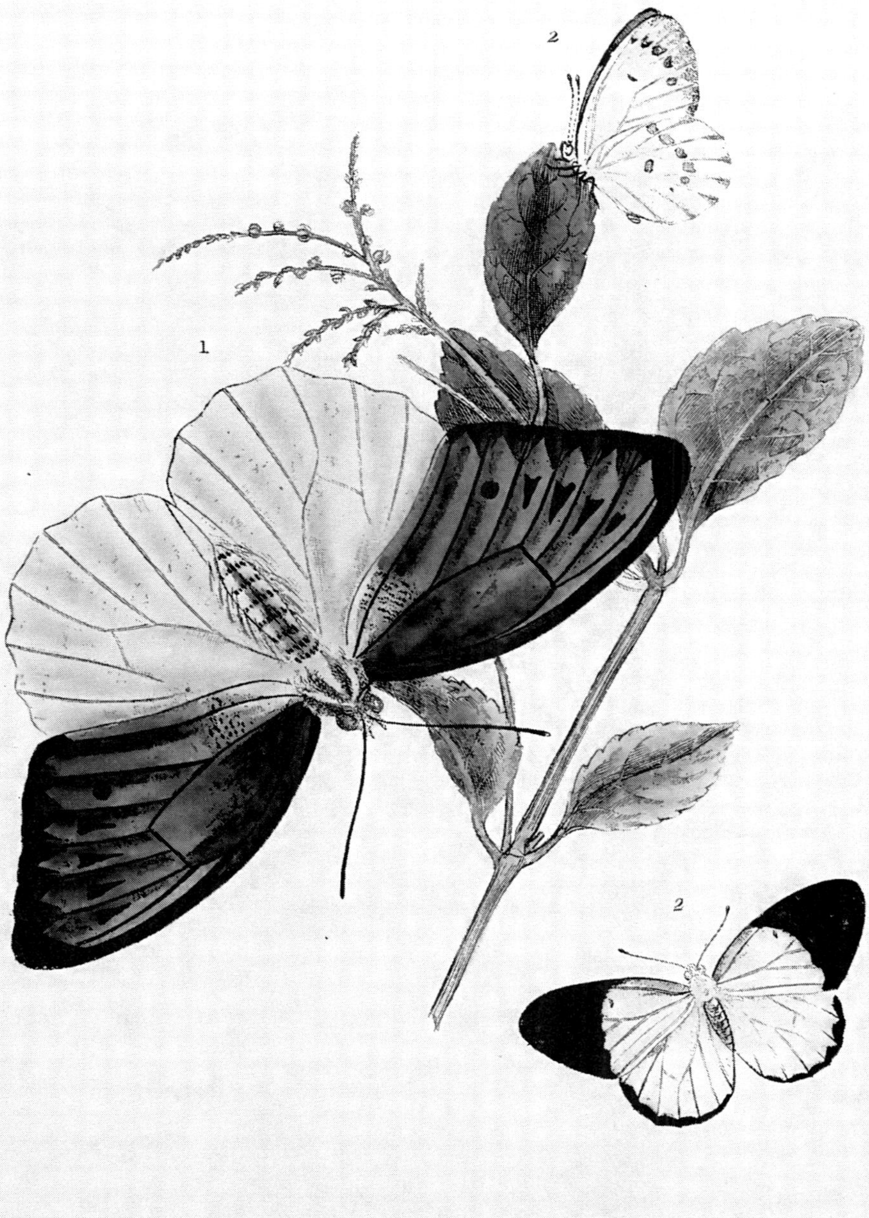

1. Pieris Leucippe. 2 Anthocharis Danæ.

PL. XXVII

1. Goniapteryx Marula. 2 Pieris Judith. 3. P. Libythea.
4. Anthocharis Eucharis 5. A. Genulia.

LEPIDOPTERA.

ANTHOCHARIS DANAE.

Plate XXVI. fig. 2.

GENUS. ANTHOCHARIS, *Boisduval.* (Pontia p. *Horsf.* Pieris p. *Enc. Méth.*)

SPECIES. ANTHOCHARIS DANAE: alis rotundatis albis; anticis apice coccineis, margine fasciaque nigris; singulis subtus striga moniliformi punctorum subferruginea abbreviata. Expans. alar. unc. 2.

ANTHOCHARIS: with the wings rounded and white; the anterior with a large apical spot of red crimson-pink, surrounded with black; beneath all the wings have a short row of dull moniliform spots. Expanse of the wings, 2 inches.

SYN. Papilio (D. C.) Danae, *Fab. Ent. Syst.* III. 1, *p.* 203. *Syst. Ent. p.* 476. *Enc. Méth.* 9. 124. (Pieris D.) *Boisduval Lepid.* i. 570. (Anthocharis D.) *Horsfield Lep. Jav. p.* 141.

Papilio Eburia, *Cramer Pap. pl.* 352, *fig. C, D, E, F.*

HABITAT. "India orientali," (*Fabricius*). Bengal, and the Cape of Good Hope, (*Boisduval*). Mysore, (*Donovan*).

GONIAPTERYX MÆRULA.

Plate XXVII. fig. 1.

FAMILY. PAPILIONIDÆ, *Leach.*

GENUS. GONIAPTERYX, *Westwood.* Gonepteryx, *Leach, Curt. Steph.* Colias, *Latr.* Rhodocera, *Boisduval Dup.*

SPECIES. GONIAPTERYX MÆRULA: alis angulatis flavis; anticis supra puncto medio atro; singulis subtus disco macula ocellari oblongo. Expans. alar. unc. 3, lin. 4.

GONIAPTERYX: with angulated yellow wings; the anterior with a central black spot on the upper side; all the wings beneath with an oblong ocellated discoidal spot. Expanse of the wings, $3\frac{1}{2}$ inches.

SYN. Papilio (Dan.) Mærula, *Fabricius Ent. Syst.* III. 1. *p.* 212. *Ent. Syst. p.* 479. *Boisduval Hist. Nat. Lepid.* 1, *p.* 600. (Rhodocera M.) *Enc. Méth.* 9. 89. (Colias M.) *Boisdv. et Leconte, Icon. Lep. Am. Sept. pl.* 23.

Papilio Ecclipsis, *Cramer, pl.* 129, *f. A, B.*

Fabricius gave "India" as the habitat of this species, whence Donovan introduced it into this work. It is now, however, well ascertained that it, as well as all the other species of the same genus, (except the British G. Rhamni,) are inhabitants of the New World. Jamaica, and Florida, are given as its true habitats by Boisduval, and New York is added in the Encyclopédie Méthodique.

M. Boisduval's grounds for substituting his own generic name, Rhodocera, in preference to that of Dr. Leach, are quite untenable; Dr. Leach's name having a long priority over that of Latreille, employed for Noctua, Libatrix, which had also been previously named Scoliopteryx by Germar, which name Stephens has retained. I have been compelled, however, slightly to alter Dr. Leach's name, to render it more in accordance with its Greek derivatives.

PIERIS JUDITH.

Plate XXVII. fig. 2.

SPECIES. PIERIS JUDITH: alis rotundatis integerrimis; anticis albis venis margineque postico (albo maculato) nigris; posticis fulvis, margine nigris. Expans. alar unc. 2—2½.

PIERIS: with the wings entire and rounded; the anterior white, with the veins and posterior margin, black, the latter spotted with white; the posterior wings fulvous, with a black border. Expanse of the wings, 2—2½ inches.

SYN. Papilio (Dan. Cand.) Judith, *Fabr. Ent. Syst.* III. 1. *p.* 202. *Boisduval Hist. Nat. Lepid.* 1. 468. *Enc. Méth.* 9. 121. *Hubner Züt.* 669—670. (Acræa J.) *Horsfield Lep. Jav. p.* 144. Pontia J.)

HABITAT. "Poulicandor, *Mus. D. Banks.*" (*Fabricius*). Java, Sumatra, (*Boisduval.*)

PIERIS LIBYTHEA.

Plate XXVII. fig. 3.

SPECIES. PIERIS LIBYTHEA: alis rotundatis integerrimis albis; anticis costa baseos apiceque, posticis punctis marginalibus fuscis. Expans. alar. unc. 2⅛.

PIERIS: with the wings entire, rounded, and white; the anterior having the costa at the base and the extremity, and the posterior having several marginal spots dark brown. Expanse of the wings, 2⅛ inches.

SYN. Papilio (Dan. Cand.) Libythea, *Fab. Ent. Syst.* III. 1. *p.* 190. *Syst. Ent. p.* 471. Pieris Libitina, *Enc. Méth.* 9. 133. *Boisduval Hist. Nat. Lepid. p.* 499.

The Fabrician *specific* name of this insect has been altered in the Encyclopédie Méthodique, merely because the same name has been *subsequently* used *generically* for a distinct group of Lepidoptera.

LEPIDOPTERA.

ANTHOCARIS EUCHARIS.

Plate XXVII. fig. 4.

SPECIES. ANTHOCARIS EUCHARIS: alis rotundatis integerrimis albis; anticis apice fulvis margine nigro; posticis immaculatis seu punctis marginalibus nigris, his infra macula costali subferruginea. Expans. alar. unc. 1½.

ANTHOCARIS: with the wings rounded, entire, and white; the anterior fulvous at the tips, with a black margin; the posterior without spots, or with small marginal black points, the latter beneath, with a small reddish costal spot. Expanse of the wings, 1½ inch.

SYN. Papilio Eucharis, *Fabr. Syst. Ent. p.* 472. *Ent. Syst.* III. 1, *p.* 195. *Enc. Méth.* 9. 124. *Boisduval Hist. Nat. Lepid. p.* 568. (Anthocaris E.)

Papilio Aurora, *Cramer, pl.* 299, *f. A, B, C, D.*

Pieris Titea, *Enc. Méth.* 9. 124. *Horsfield Lep. Jav. p.* 141.

HABITAT. "India orientali," (*Fabricius*). Coromandel, Pegu, (*Boisduval*).

ANTHOCARIS GENUTIA.

Plate XXVII. fig. 5.

SPECIES. ANTHOCARIS GENUTIA: alis falcatis, integerrimis, albis; anticis apice fulvis; posticis punctis marginalibus nigris, subtus viridi marmoratis. Expans. alar unc. 1½.

ANTHOCARIS: with the wings entire, white; the anterior falcate, with the tip fulvous; the posterior with marginal black spots, and on the under side marbled with green. Expanse of the wings, 1½ inch.

SYN. Papilio (Dan. Cand.) Genutia, *Fabricius Ent. Syst.* III. 1, *p.* 193. (*nec* Pap. Genutia *Cramer, pl.* 206, *f. C, D.*) *Enc. Méth.* 9, *p.* 168, (Pieris G.) *p.* 806, (Libythea G.) *Boisduval Hist. Nat. Lepid.* 1. 565.

Mancipium vorax Medea, *Hubn. Exot. Samml.*

♀ Pieris L'Herminieri, *Enc. Méth.* 9. 167.

There appears to have been two errors committed respecting this insect. In the first place, it is evidently very closely allied to the orange-tipped butterfly of our country, (Anthocharis Cardamines); the palpi, as represented in this figure, are fictitious, being elongated like those of the genus Libythea, which induced M. Godart to place it in that genus, in the appendix to his article on the butterflies in the Encyclopédie Méthodique. In the second place, instead of being an inhabitant of the East Indies, as stated by Fabricius, (and on his authority introduced into this work,) it is now known to belong to North America: a species agreeing in all respects with the

Fabrician insect, but with ordinary sized palpi, having been since discovered in North America, and described in the Encyclopédie Méthodique, under the name of Pieris L'Herminieri.

PIERIS AMARYLLIS.

Plate XXVIII. fig. 1.

SPECIES. PIERIS AMARYLLIS: alis rotundatis, integerrimis, concoloribus, obscure albis; anticis utrinque lunula media nigra. Expans. alar. unc. $2\frac{3}{4}$.

PIERIS: with the wings rounded, entire, concolorous, dirty white; the anterior pair having a small central black lunule visible both above and beneath. Expanse of the wings, $2\frac{3}{4}$ inches.

SYN. Papilio (Dan. Cand.) Amaryllis, *Fabr. Ent. Syst.* III. 1, *p.* 189. *Enc. Méth.* 9. 141. *Boisduval Hist. Nat. Lep.* 1. *p.* 549.

M. Boisduval expresses a doubt whether this species be really an inhabitant of the East Indies.

PIERIS CASTALIA.

Plate XXVIII. fig. 2.

SPECIES. PIERIS CASTALIA: alis integerrimis, rotundatis, albis, supra immaculatis subtus basi flavescentibus. Expans. alar. unc. $2\frac{1}{4}$.

PIERIS: with the wings entire, rounded, and white, without any spots above, but with the base of the wings yellowish beneath. Expanse of the wings, $2\frac{1}{4}$ inches.

SYN. Papilio (Dan. Cand.) Castalia, *Fabr. Ent. Syst.* III. 1. *p.* 188. *Enc. Méth.* 9. 160. (Pieris C.) *Boisduval Hist. Nat. Lepid. p.* 516.

COLIAS (CALLIDRYAS) SCYLLA.

Plate XXVIII. fig. 3.

GENUS. COLIAS, *Latreille et Godart.* (SUBGENUS: Callidryas, *Boisduval.*)

SPECIES. COLIAS (CALLIDRYAS) SCYLLA: alis integerrimis subrotundatis, supra anticis albis limbo nigro, posticis aurantiacis; subtus omnibus nebulosis. Expans. alar. $2\frac{1}{2}$.

COLIAS (CALLIDRYAS): with the wings entire and rounded, above the anterior are white, with a black posterior border, and the posterior are rich orange; beneath all the wings are mottled with yellowish. Expanse of the wings, $2\frac{1}{2}$ inches.

Pl. XXVIII

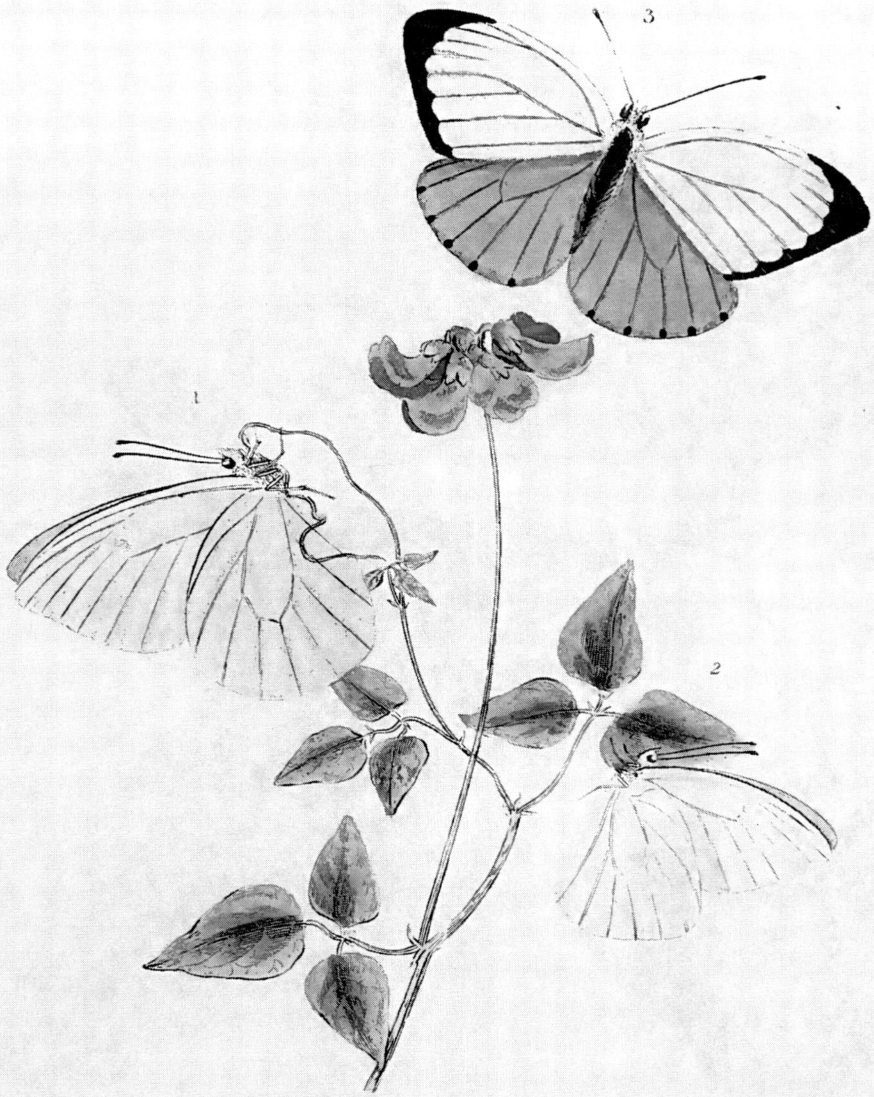

1. Pieris Amaryllis. 2. Pieris Castalia.

3. Colias Scylla.

Pl. XXI.

1. Vanessa Cacta 2. Nymphalis Pelarius.

3. Nymphalis Athamas

1. *Morpho Menetho.* 2 *Hipparchia? Arcesilaus.*
3. *Nymphalis orsis* 4 *N. Liberia.*

Syn. Papilio (Dan. Cand.) Scylla, *Linn. Syst. Nat.* 2. 763. *Fabr. Ent. Syst.* III, 1. *p.* 201. *Cramer, tab.* 12, *f. C, D.* (♂) *Sulzer Gesch. Ins. t.* 15, *f.* 6. *Enc. Méth.* 9. 95. *Boisduval Hist. Nat. Lep. p.* 631.

♂ Papilio Cornelia, *Fabr. Mant.* 2. *p.* 21.

Colias Scylla, *Horsfield Lep. Jav. p.* 133, *pl.* 4, *f.* 6, (larva and pupa.)

The caterpillar of this very distinct species, according to Dr. Horsfield, is very common in the eastern part of Java upon the Cassia fistula and obtusifolia. It is extremely abundant, particularly in the early part of the rainy season, after the renewal of the foliage of these plants. It is green, with minute black tubercles arranged in transverse series, and with a lateral yellow line above the legs. The chrysalis is boat-shaped, with the head pointed, but not so much elevated as some other species of this genus.

The last three species are represented on Dolichos lignosus.

VANESSA CACTA.

Plate XXIX. fig. 1.

Species. Vanessa Cacta: alis angulato-dentatis, anticis nigris basi purpureis macula magna transversa fulva, posticis fuscis strigis duabus submarginalibus. Expans. alar. unc. $2\frac{1}{2}$.

Vanessa: with the wings angulato-dentated, the anterior black, with the basal portion purple, and with a large transverse orange spot; the posterior brown with two submarginal black lines. Expanse of the wings, $2\frac{1}{2}$ inches.

Syn. Papilio (Nymphalis) Cacta, *Fabr. Ent. Syst.* III. 1, *p.* 116. *Enc. Méth.* 9. 309.

Originally described by Fabricius from the collection and drawings of Mr. Jones, from which Donovan most probably also obtained the present figure.

NYMPHALIS OCTAVIUS.

Plate XXIX. fig. 2.

Species. Nymphalis Octavius: alis nigris, fascia lata communi viridi, antice abbreviata, posticis caudatis; subtus griseis striga fusca. Expans. alar. unc. $2\frac{1}{2}$.

Nymphalis: with black wings, a broad green bar running across them, not extending to the anterior margin of the anterior pair; posterior pair tailed; beneath grey with a brown streak. Expanse of the wings, $2\frac{1}{2}$ inches.

Syn. Papilio (N.) Octavius, *Fabr. Ent. Syst.* III. 1. *p.* 73. (*nec* P. Octavia, *p.* 120.) *Enc. Méth.* 9. 368. (Nymphalis D.)

Fabricius gave India as the habitat of this species, but in the Encyclopédie Méthodique it is said to be from South America, being in that work doubtfully regarded as the female of the Brazilian species Nymphalis Iphis of Humboldt and Bonpland's voyage, which is therein considered as identical with the Papilio (N.) Morvus of Fabricius, by whom also India is given as the habitat of the last named species.

NYMPHALIS (CHARAXES) ATHAMAS.

Plate XXIX. fig. 3.

Genus. Nymphalis, *Latreille.* Papilio, (Nymphalis p.) *Fabricius.* (Subgenus: Charaxes, *Boisduval.* Jasia, *Swainson.*)

Species, Nymphalis (Charaxes) Athamas: alis supra nigris, utrinque fascia media lata glauca subhyalinâ, subtus lunulis ferrugineis marginata. Expans. alar. unc. 3.

Nymphalis: with the wings above black, on each side with a broad central glaucous subhyaline bar, which on the underside is margined with ferruginous lunules. Expanse of the wings, 3 inches.

Syn. Papilio (Equit. Ach.) Athamas, *Drury, vol.* 1, *pl.* 2, *fig.* 4. *Cramer Pap. pl.* 89, *f. C, D. Enc. Méth.* 9. 353. (Nymphalis A.)

Papilio Pyrrhus, *Donovan,* 1*st edit.* (excl. Syn. *Linn.*)

MORPHO MENETHO.

Plate XXX. fig. 1.

Genus. Morpho, *Fabricius, Latreille, Godart.*

Species. Morpho Menetho: alis dentatis fuscis, strigis duabus submarginalibus macularum flavarum, subtus flavescentibus, fasciis duabus fuscis. Expans. alar. unc. $3\frac{3}{4}$.

Morpho: with brown dentated wings, and with two rows of submarginal yellow spots, beneath yellowish with two brown fasciæ. Expanse of the wings, $3\frac{3}{4}$ inches.

Syn. Papilio (Nymph.) Menctho, *Fabr. Ent. Syst.* III. 1, *p.* 83. *Enc. Méth.* 9. 446.

This insect is nearly allied to Morpho Tullia, *Fabricius.* The present figure does not precisely agree with the Fabrician description; but as both were, in all probability, derived from the same source, Mr. Jones's collection of drawings, there can be but little doubt upon their identity.

LEPIDOPTERA.

HIPPARCHIA? ARCESILAUS.

Plate XXX. fig. 2.

GENUS. HIPPARCHIA, *Fabricius*. Satyrus, *Latreille, Godart*.

SPECIES. HIPPARCHIA? ARCESILAUS: alis integerrimis, supra ferrugineis immaculatis, subtus fuscis strigis duabus obscurioribus. Expans. alar. unc. 2⅙.

HIPPARCHIA? with entire wings, above ferruginous immaculate, beneath brown with two darker parallel streaks. Expanse of the wings, 2⅙ inches.

SYN. Papilio (Nymph.) Arcesilaus, *Fabr. Ent. Syst.* III. 1. *p.* 153. *Enc. Méth.* 9. 497. (Satyrus? A.) (*nec* Pap. Arcesilaus, *Cramer, pl.* 294.)

HABITAT "Siam, *Mus. Dom. Banks*," (*Fabricius*).

Fabricius is silent regarding the submarginal row of white dots represented in this figure.

NYMPHALIS ORSIS.

♀ Plate XXX. fig. 3.

SPECIES. NYMPHALIS: alis nigris, (in mare cæruleo micantibus) strigis tribus macularibus, posticis striga marginali cærulea. Expans. alar. unc. 2½.

NYMPHALIS: with the wings black, (in the male shining blue) with three transverse rows of white spots, and with a submarginal blue streak on the posterior wings. Expanse of the wings, 2½ inches.

SYN. Papilio (Nymph. Phal.) Orsis, *Drury Illustr. vol.* 3, *pl.* 16, *f.* 3.
Papilio (N.) Oisis, *Fabr. Ent. Syst.* III. 1. *p.* 124. ♂. *Enc. Méth.* 9. 381.
Papilio (N.) Blandina, *Fab. Ent. Syst.* III. 1. *p.* 129. ♀. *Donovan*, 1*st edit.*

This Brazilian insect was probably introduced into this work in consequence of the vague expression of Fabricius, "Habitat in Indiis," which was applied not only to N. Blandina, (or the female), but also to N. Orsis, (or the male.)

NYMPHALIS LIBERIA.

Plate XXX. fig. 4.

SPECIES. NYMPHALIS LIBERIA: alis dentatis, supra fulvis, anticarum arca apicis obscura; posticis supra puncto atro, subtus tribus ocellaribus. Expans. alar. unc. 2.

NYMPHALIS: with the wings dentated, above fulvous, the anterior with a dark coloured curved mark near the tips, the posterior with a single black dot above, and with three ocellated spots beneath. Expanse of the wings, 2 inches.

SYN. Papilio (Nymph.) Liberia, *Fabr. Ent. Syst.* III. 1. *p.* 135. *Enc. Meth.* 9. 375.

The same observation may be applied to this South American species as to the last,—Stoll, who investigated the transformations of many of the Lepidoptera of Guiana, having described its preparatory states. The caterpillar is of a dark green colour, with the head blue, and the legs and anal fork yellow. It is armed with black branching spines, of which the two anterior ones are by far the longest. The chrysalis is elongated, with the head bifid, and of a green colour. It appears to be a very variable species, as the Papilio Agatha and Merione of Fabricius, P. Laothoe of Herbst, and P. Ariadne of Cramer, are referred to it in the Encyclopédie Méthodique.

NYMPHALIS? PHEGEA.

Plate XXXI. fig. 1.

SPECIES. NYMPHALIS? PHEGEA: alis dentatis fuscis, nigro undatis, anticis fascia maculari, posticis disco ferrugineo aut albo; subtus pallidioribus. Expans. alar. unc. $3\frac{3}{4}$.

NYMPHALIS? with the wings dentated, brown, with numerous black waves; the anterior with a row of spots, and the disc of the posterior wings of a ferruginous or white colour; beneath the wings are paler, and the black waves more distinct. Expanse of the wings, $3\frac{3}{4}$ inches.

SYN. Papilio (N.) Phegea, *Fabr. Ent. Syst.* III. 1. *p.* 132. *Enc Meth.* 9. 406, (Nymphalus? P.)

NYMPHALIS FATIMA.

Plate XXXI. fig. 2.

SPECIES. NYMPHALIS FATIMA: alis atris, fascia communi flava, posticarum abbreviata; anticis punctis quatuor flavis subapicalibus; posticis maculis rubris mediis, subcaudatis. Expans. alar unc. $2\frac{1}{2}$.

NYMPHALIS: with the wings black, having a yellow bar running across them, which is abbreviated in the posterior pair; the anterior having also four subapical yellow spots, and the posterior several red spots in the middle, the latter slightly tailed. Expanse of the wings, $2\frac{1}{2}$ inches.

Pl. XXXI

1. *Nymphalis? Phegea* 2. *N. Fatima* 3. *Argynnis Thyelia*

PL. XXX

1. *Pieris Neropl.* 2. *Nymphalis Gnidia*
3. *Biblis Hiarbas.*

SYN. Papilio (Nymph.) Fatima, *Fabr. Ent. Syst.* III. 1. *p.* 81. *Enc. Méth.* 9. 375, (Nymphalis F.)

Fabricius gives the habitat of this species "in Indiis," with the observation, that it is of the figure of the South American Papilio Iphicla. (*Drury,* 1. *pl.* 14, *f.* 3, 4.) Hence I think it most probable that the term must be considered to signify the West Indies, or South America, and that the species is incorrectly introduced into the present work.

ARGYNNIS THYELIA.

Plate XXXI. fig. 3.

GENUS. ARGYNNIS, *Fabricius, Latreille, Godart.* ARGYREUS, *Scop.*

SPECIES. ARGYNNIS THYELIA: alis subrotundatis subdentatis, supra fulvis extimo maculisque nigris; posticis subtus pallidè testaceis fascia alba, transversa, media, punctis duobus baseos roseis nigroque cinctis. Expan. alar. $2\frac{1}{3}$ unc.

ARGYNNIS: with the wings rather rounded and dentate, above fulvous, with the tip and several spots black; the posterior beneath pale brick red, with a white bar across the middle, and with two crimson basal spots, bordered with black. Expanse of the wings, $2\frac{1}{3}$ inches.

SYN. Papilio (N.) Thyelia, *Fab. Ent. Syst.* III. 1. *p.* 142. *Enc. Méth.* 9. 257. (Argynnis T.)

PIERIS NERO.

Plate XXXII. fig. 1.

SPECIES. PIERIS NERO: alis integerrimis, anticis elongato-trigonis, sanguineis, margine parum fuscescente, subtus aurantiis; posticis strigis duobus fuscis fere obsoletis. Expans. alar. unc. 3.

PIERIS: with the wings entire, the anterior elongate-trigonate, sanguineous, with the nerves and margin brownish, beneath orange; the posterior wings with two nearly obsolete streaks. Expanse of the wings, 3 inches.

SYN. Papilio (Nymph.) Nero, *Fabricius Ent. Syst.* III. 1. *p.* 153. *Enc. Méth.* 9. 805, *Supp.* (Pieris N.) *Boisduval Hist. Nat. Lepid.* 1. 485.

Pieris Thyria, *Enc. Méth.* 9, 147. *Guerin Icon. R. An. Ins. pl.* 77, *f.* 1. *Horsfield, Zool. Jour. vol.* 4, *pl.* 4, *f.* 2.

HABITAT. "In Asia, *Mus. Britann.*" (*Fabricius*). Java, (*Horsfield, Boisduval*).

NYMPHALIS GNIDIA.

Plate XXXII. fig. 2.

SPECIES. NYMPHALES GNIDIA: alis dentatis testaceis; anticis apice fuscis fascia media punctisque subapicalibus albis; posticis striga fulva, lunulis nigris. Expans. alar. unc. 2½.

NYMPHALIS: with the wings dentated testaceous; the anterior with the extremity brown, with a white central fascia, and several subapical white spots; the posterior with a submarginal fulvous band with black lunules. Expanse of the wings, 2½ inches.

SYN. Papilio (N.) Gnidia, *Fabr. Ent. Syst.* III. 1, *p.* 137. *Enc. Méth.* 9. 386? (Nymphalis G.?)

HABITAT. "In Indiis," (*Fabricius*).

Described by Fabricius from the collection and drawings of Mr. Jones, which also, in all probability, supplied the accompanying figure.

BIBLIS HIARBAS.

Plate XXXII. fig. 3.

GENUS. BIBLIS, *Fabricius, Latreille, Godart.* Papilio, *Donovan.*

SPECIES. BIBLIS HIARBAS: alis dentatis, fuscis; fascia utrinque communi alba, posticarum latiore, anticarum abbreviata; marginibus lunulis rufis. Expans. alar. unc. 2½.

BIBLIS: with the wings dentated, brown, with a white fascia running through the wings both above and beneath; being narrower and abbreviated in the anterior pair; the margins of the wings with red lunules. Expanse of the wings, 2½ inches.

SYN. Papilio (N.) Hiarbas, *Drury Illustr. vol.* 3, *pl.* 14. *Fabr. Ent. Syst.* III. 1, *p.* 128. (Papilio (N.) Hiarba). *Enc. Méth.* 9. 824. (Biblis Hiarba.)

Drury, to whom Fabricius was indebted for his knowledge of this species, states that he received it from Sierra Leone. Fabricius, however, gave his usual vague locality, "In Indiis," upon which authority Donovan introduced it into this work. It is, however, a widely distributed African insect, being found in the country of the Hottentots, (*Enc. Méth.*) and having been received by me from the Cape of Good Hope.

PL. XXXIII

1. Nymphalis Isis. 2 Nymphalis Phorcys.
3. N. Eribotes 4. N. Isidore.

LEPIDOPTERA.

NYMPHALIS ISIS.

Plate XXXIII. fig. 1.

SPECIES. NYMPHALIS ISIS: alis fusco-nigris, anticis integris, utrinque macula disci chermesina; posticis dentatis supra striga marginali albida; omnibus subtus viridi-lineatis. Expans. alar. unc. $2\frac{1}{2}$.

NYMPHALIS: with blackish brown wings; the anterior entire with a large discoidal sanguineous spot; the posterior dentated, with a whitish marginal streak; all the wings beneath with green lines. Expanse of the wings, $2\frac{1}{2}$ inches.

SYN. Papilio (Dan. Fest.) Isis, *Drury, vol.* 3, *pl.* 7, *f.* 1, 2. *Fab. Ent. Syst.* III. 1. *p.* 124. *Enc. Méth.* 9. 421. (Nymphalis I.)

The Fabrician expression, "In Indiis," indicating the habitat of this species, has evidently again induced our author to give this insect a place in these Illustrations. That it is an inhabitant of Brazil, we have the authority both of Drury, and the Encyclopédie Méthodique.

NYMPHALIS PHORCYS.

Plate XXXIII. fig. 2.

SPECIES. NYMPHALIS PHORCYS: alis dentato-subcaudatis, supra fuscis immaculatis, subtus obscurius strigosis; posticis punctis duobus cinereis. Expans. alar. unc. $2\frac{3}{4}$.

NYMPHALIS: with the wings dentate, slightly tailed, the upper side brown immaculate, beneath with several obscure slender streaks; the posterior also with two ashy-coloured spots. Expanse of the wings, $2\frac{3}{4}$ inches.

SYN. Papilio (N.) Phorcys, *Fabr. Ent. Syst.* III. 1, *p.* 80. *Enc. Méth.* 9. 372.

NYMPHALIS ERIBOTES.

Plate XXXIII. fig. 3.

SPECIES. NYMPHALIS ERIBOTES: alis subcaudatis, fulvis aut ferrugineis, basi violaceo micantibus, subtus griseis. Expans. alar. unc. $2\frac{3}{4}$.

NYMPHALIS: with the wings slightly tailed, above fulvous or ferruginous, with the base shining with violet or purple; all the wings beneath greyish. Expanse of the wings, $2\frac{3}{4}$ inches.

SYN. Papilio (N.) Eribotes, *Fabr. Syst. Ent. p.* 484. *Ent. Syst.* III. 1. *p.* 73. *Enc. Méth.* 9. 316, (Nymphalis E.)

Papilio Leonida, *Cramer, pl.* 338, *f. C, D.* *Stoll Suppl. Cramer, pl.* 6 *f.* 2, *A, B.* (larva et pupa.)

Fabricius described this insect from the collection of Dr. Hunter, now belonging to the University of Glasgow, and gave its habitat "In India." It is, however, a native of Guiana, in South America, Stoll having reared it from the caterpillar state in that country. The caterpillar is black, with short hairs, and a great number of white dots. The chrysalis is short, without angular projections, of a grey colour, and is found suspended by its tail from the twigs of the shrubs upon which the larva had been nourished. In the description given in the Encyclopédie Méthodique, the anal angle of the posterior wings is described as being ornamented with four or five small black and white spots, of which no mention is made by Fabricius, nor are they indicated in the accompanying figure.

NYMPHALIS ISIDORE.

Plate XXXIII. fig. 4.

SPECIES. NYMPHALIS ISIDORE: alis anticis falcatis, posticis caudatis; omnibus fulvis, anticis punctis duobus mediis pallidis, macula costali apiceque fuscis. Expans. alar. unc. 3.

NYMPHALIS: with the anterior wings falcate, the posterior tailed; all the wings above fulvous, the anterior with two pale spots on the middle, and with a costal spot, and the extremity brown. Expanse of the wings, 3 inches.

SYN. Papilio Isidore, *Cramer Pap. pl.* 235, *fig. A, B, E, F.* *Herbst. Pap. t.* 150, *f.* 1, 2. *Enc. Méth.* 9. 371. (Nymphalis I.)

Fabricius again uses the expression "In Indiis," to designate the habitat of this species, which, in the Encyclopédie Méthodique is stated to be an inhabitant of Guiana and Brazil.

CETHOSIA CYDIPPE.

♂ Plate XXXIV. fig. 1.

GENUS. CETHOSIA, *Fabricius, Latreille, Godart.*

SPECIES. CETHOSIA CYDIPPE: alis dentatis, basi rufis, apice nigris, lunulis subapicalibus serie duplici digestis albis; anticis fascia lata abbreviata pone medium; subtus basi testaceis nigro cæruleoque variis. Expans. alar. unc. 4¼.

CETHOSIA: with the wings dentated, the base red, and the tips black, with white lunules arranged in a double series within the exterior margins; the anterior having

PL. XXXIV

1. Cethosia Cydippe. 2. Nymphalis Dirce
3. Nymphalis Euronimene.

also a broad short white fascia beyond the middle; beneath at the base testaceous, with black and blue markings. Expanse of the wings, 4¼ inches.

SYN. Papilio Cydippe, *Linn. Syst. Nat.* 2. 776. *Fabr. Ent. Syst.* III. 1. *p.* 112. *Clerck Icon. tab.* 36, *f.* 1. *Herbst, Pap. t.* 245, *f.* 4, 5.

Papilio Iris, *Cramer Pap. pl.* 62, *fig. A, B.*

HABITAT. "In India," (*Linnæus.*) In China, (*Enc. Méth.*)

NYMPHALIS DIRCE.

Plate XXXIV. fig. 2.

SPECIES. NYMPHALIS DIRCE: alis fuscis, anticis utrinque fascia flava; subtus omnibus albido nigroque striatis; posticis angulatis. Expans. alar. unc. 2—3.

NYMPHALIS: with the wings brown, the anterior on both sides with a broad oblique yellow band; beneath all the wings striped with pale buff and brownish black; the posterior wings angulated. Expanse of the wings, 2 to 3 inches.

SYN. Papilio Dirce, *Linn. Syst. Nat.* 2. 778. *Cramer, pl.* 212, *f. C, D. Stoll Suppl. Cramer, pl.* 2, *f.* 3, *A, B,* 4, *A, B. Fabr. Ent. Syst.* III. 1. *p.* 123. *Enc. Méth.* 9. 371, (Nymphalis D.)

Linnæus and Fabricius state of this species, "Habitat in Indiis." It is, however, an inhabitant of Guiana and Brazil, Stoll having reared it in that country; the caterpillar is black.

NYMPHALIS EURINOME.

Plate XXXIV. fig. 3.

SPECIES. NYMPHALIS EURINOME: alis subdentatis, nigris, maculis permultis posticarumque disco baseos albis. Expans. alar. unc. 3¾.

NYMPHALIS: with the wings slightly dentate, black, with a considerable number of spots, and the basal disc of the posterior wings white. Expanse of the wings, 3¾ inches.

SYN. Papilio Eurinome, *Cramer Pap. tab.* 70, *fig. A. Fab. Ent. Syst.* III. 1. *p.* 57. *Enc. Méth.* 9. 398.

HABITAT. In India orientali.

NYMPHALIS HIPPONA.

Plate XXXV. fig. 1.

SPECIES. NYMPHALIS HIPPONA: alis supra nigris; anticis fulvo flavoque variis; posticis caudatis, basi fulvo, apice nigro striga marginali lunularum albarum. Expans. alar. unc. 4.

NYMPHALIS: with the wings black above; the anterior varied with fulvous and yellow; the posterior with a long tail, the base fulvous, the apex black, with a row of marginal white lunules. Expanse of the wings, 4 inches.

SYN. Papilio (N.) Hippona, *Fabr. Sp. Ins.* 2, *p.* 54. *Enc. Méth.* 9. 362. *Drury Illustr.* (2*d edit.*) *vol.* 3, *p.* 21.

Papilio (N.) Fabius, *Cramer Pap. pl.* 90, *fig. C, D. Stoll Suppl. Cramer, pl.* 2, *f.* 1, 1 *A*, 1 *B*, 1 *C. Drury Illustr.* (1*st edit.*) *vol.* 3, *pl.* 16, *f.* 1, 2.

Fabricius erroneously gave "India" as the habitat of this curious insect, which induced Donovan to introduce it into this work. It is, however, a native of Guiana and Brazil. Its transformations have been observed by Stoll, who has figured the insect in its different states, as above referred to. The caterpillar is dark green, with a black dorsal line and lateral black spots; the head is armed with two short obtuse spines. It feeds only by night, concealing itself by day in a rolled-up leaf; the chrysalis is short and thick, without angular projections.

CETHOSIA CYANE.

Plate XXXV. fig. 2.

SPECIES. CETHOSIA CYANE: alis dentatis, nigris, linea tenuissima angulata submarginali, anticis fascia, posticis disco (nigro-punctato) albis. Expans. alar. unc. $3\frac{1}{2}$.

CETHOSIA: with the wings dentate, black, with a very slender angulated line running within the posterior margin of the wings, the anterior having a fascia, and the poster the disc white, the latter spotted black. Expanse of the wings, $3\frac{1}{2}$ inches.

SYN. Papilio (N. P.) Cyane, *Drury, App. vol.* 2, 1*st edit. Herbst. Pap. tab.* 248, *f.* 3, 4. *Cramer Pap. pl.* 295, *f. C, D. Fabr. Ent. Syst.* III. 1. *p.* 115.

HABITAT. Bengal, (*Drury*). India, (*Fabricius*).

PL. XXXV.

1. Nymphalis Hippona. 2. Cethosia Cyane.
3. Nymphalis Coenobita.

Pl. XXXVI.

1. Nymphalis Cocalia. 3. Vanessa Sophia.
2. Hipparchia Baldus. 4. Nymphalis Auge.

LEPIDOPTERA.

NYMPHALIS CÆNOBITA.

Plate XXXV. fig. 2.

SQECIES. NYMPHALIS CÆNOBITA: alis dentatis, nigris, anticis stria maculisque, posticis supra fascia alba; subtus albis, fasciis quatuor maculisque marginalibus fuscis. Expans. alar unc. 2½.

NYMPHALIS: with the wings dentate, black; the anterior with a broad band, and numerous spots and lunules of white; the posterior above with a white fascia; beneath white with four fasciæ, and marginal spots of brown. Expanse of the wings, 2½ inches.

SYN. Papilio (N.) Cænobita, *Fabr. Ent. Syst.* III. 1. *p.* 247. *Enc. Méth.* 9. 433. (Nymphalis C.)

HABITAT. "In Indiis," (*Fabricius*).

NYMPHALIS (ACONTHEA) COCALIA.

Plate XXXVI. fig. 1.

GENUS. NYMPHALIS, *Latreille, Godart.* (SUBGENUS: Aconthea, *Horsfield.*)

SPECIES. NYMPHALIS (ACONTHEA) COCALIA: alis dentatis, fuscis; anticis nigro flavoque maculatis; subtus omnibus griseis striga punctorum alborum. Expans. alar. unc. 3.

NYMPHALIS (ACONTHEA): with the wings dentated, brown; the anterior varied with black and buff spots; beneath all the wings are grey, with a row of white spots. Expanse of the wings, 3 inches.

SYN. Papilio (N.) Cocalia, *Fabr. Ent. Syst.* III. 1. *p.* 250. *Enc. Méth.* 9. 405. (Nymphalis C.) *nec* Papilio Cocala, *Herbst et Cramer*.

HIPPARCHIA BALDUS.

Plate XXXVI. fig. 2.

SPECIES. HIPPARCHIA BALDUS: alis integerrimis, fuscis, subtus cinereo undatis; anticis utrinque ocello magno pupilla gemina; posticis supra ocellis quatuor, subtus sex. Expans. alar. unc. 1½.

HIPPARCHIA: with the wings entire, brown, beneath with grey waves; the anterior on each side with a large ocellus, having a double pupil; the posterior above, with four, beneath with six eyelets. Expanse of the wings, 1½ inch.

SYN. Papilio (Satyrus) Baldus, *Fabr. Syst. Ent.* III. 1. *p.* 223. *Enc. Méth.* 9. 551. (Satyrus B.)

Papilio Lysandra, *Cramer, pl.* 293, *fig. G, H.*

VANESSA SOPHIA.

Plate XXXVI. fig. 3.

SPECIES. VANESSA SOPHIA: alis denticulatis, anticis subfalcatis, posticis rotundatis, omnibus supra fulvo, nigro, flavidoque variis, limbo fusco nigro punctata, lunulis posticarum albis. Expans. alar. unc. $1\frac{3}{4}$—2.

VANESSA: with the wings denticulated, the anterior subfalcate, the posterior rounded above; all the wings are varied with fulvous, black, and buff, with a broad brown border with black spots, and with submarginal white lunules in the posterior wings. Expanse of the wings, $1\frac{3}{4}$ to 2 inches.

SYN. Papilio (Satyrus) Sophia, *Fabr. Ent. Syst.* III. 1. *p.* 248. *Enc. Méth.* 9. 823.

Fabricius described this species from the collection of Mr. Drury, and the drawings of Mr. Jones, with the habitat "In Indiis." In the Encyclopédie Méthodique, the western coast of Africa is stated to be its native country.

NYMPHALIS AUGE.

Pl. XXXVI. fig. 4.

SPECIES. NYMPHALIS AUGE: alis dentatis, fuscis; anticis fasciis tribus viridibus; posticis fulvis serie submarginali punctorum nigrorum. Expans. alar. unc. $1\frac{5}{6}$.

NYMPHALIS: with the wings dentated, brown; the anterior with three greenish fasciæ, the posterior fulvous with a submarginal row of black spots. Expanse of the wings, $1\frac{5}{6}$ inch.

SYN. Papilio (Satyrus) Auge, *Fabr. Ent. Syst.* III. 1. *p.* 248. *Enc. Méth.* 9. 387.

This insect is also stated by Fabricius to have been in the collection of Mr. Drury, and figured by Mr. Jones, and the habitat is also given "In Indiis." From its near relationship, however, with N. Sophia and N. Doriclea, both of which are inhabitants of western tropical Africa, I have little doubt that N. Auge is from that quarter of the globe, and not from either of the Indies.

NYMPHALIS PERIANDER.

Plate XXXVII. fig. 1.

SPECIES. NYMPHALIS PERIANDER: alis utrinque albis, strigis sex flavescentibus, margine postico fusco albo strigoso; posticis caudatis. Expans. alar. unc. $1\frac{3}{4}$.

PL. XXXVII

1. Nymphalis Periander. 2. Erycina Attica?
3. N. Anova. 4. Hipparchia Crantor. 5. N. Lirissa.

NYMPHALIS: with the wings on both sides white with six yellow stripes, posterior margin brown with white lines; posterior wings tailed. Expanse of the wings, 1¾ inch.

SYN. Papilio (N.) Periander, *Fabr. Ent. Syst.* III. 1. *p.* 67. *Enc. Méth.* 9. 362. (Nymphalis P.) *Horsfield Lep. Jav. pl.* 5, *f.* 3, and 3 *a.* (Paphia P.)

HABITAT. Mysore, (*Donovan*). Java, (*Enc. Méth.*)

ERYCINA (ZEMEROS) ALLICA.

Pl. XXXVII. fig. 2.

FAMILY. LYCÆNIDÆ, *Leach.*

GENUS. ERYCINA, *Fabricius, Latreille, Godart.* (SUBGENUS: Zemeros, *Boisduval.*)

SPECIES. ERYCINA (ZEMEROS) ALLICA: alis denticulatis obscure fulvis, punctis nigris numerosis, albo fœtis. Expans. alar. unc. 1½.

ERYCINA (ZEMEROS): with denticulated wings of an obscure fulvous colour, with numerous black spots, accompanied with smaller white ones. Expanse of the wings, 1½ inch.

SYN. Papilio (S.) Allica, *Fabr. Ent. Syst.* III. 1. *p.* 244. *Enc. Méth.* 9. 567. (Erycina A.) *Boisduval Hist. Nat. Lepid.* 1, *pl.* 21, *fig.* 5. (Zemeros A.)

HABITAT. Siam, (*Fabricius*). China, Bengal, Java, (*Enc. Méth.*)

NYMPHALIS ANCÆAS.

♂ Pl. XXXVII. fig. 3.

SPECIES. NYMPHALIS ANCÆAS: alis supra atris (♂), aut fuscis, (♀); anticarum fascia cyanea obliqua, posticarum (♂) macula magna discoidali rufa; subtus viridibus, posticarum strigis tribus ferrugineis. Expans. alar. unc. 2½.

NYMPHALIS: with the wings above black in the male, or brown in the female; the anterior with a broad oblique cyaneous or green bar, the posterior in the male with a large discoidal red spot; beneath green, the posterior with three ferrugineous streaks. Expanse of the wings, 2½ inches.

SYN. ♂ Papilio (N.) Ancæa, *Linn. Syst. Nat.* 2. 781. *Fabr. Ent. Syst.* III. *p.* 154. *Enc. Méth.* 9. 409. *Cramer Pap. pl.* 338, *fig. C, D.*

Papilio Obrinus, *Donovan*, 1*st edit.*

♀ Papilio (N.) Obrinus, *Linn. Syst. Nat.* 2. *p.* 776. *Fabr. Ent. Syst.* III. 1, *p.* 154. *Cramer Pap. pl.* 49, *fig. E, F. Stoll Suppl. Cramer, pl.* 6, *f.* 5.

Stoll, by rearing this insect in Guiana, clearly proved not only the incorrectness of the old habitat assigned to it of India, but also that the two Linnæan species,

P. Ancæa and Obrinus, were the sexes of the same species. The caterpillar, according to the first named author, is green, with a lateral line, the head ferruginous, and armed with two branching spines; its back is also armed with shorter spines. The chrysalis is grey, and is suspended by the tail.

HIPPARCHIA CRANTOR.

Pl. XXXVII. fig. 4.

SPECIES. HIPPARCHIA CRANTOR: alis integerrimis, fuscis; supra anticis immaculatis; posticis ocello unico bipupillato; subtus quinque, primo quartoque bipupillato. Expans. alar. unc. 1⅔.

HIPPARCHIA: with the wings entire, brown; the anterior immaculate above, the posterior with a single ocellus with two pupils; beneath with five ocelli, the first and fourth having two pupils. Expanse of the wings, 1⅔ inch.

SYN. Papilio (N.) Crantor, *Fabr. Ent. Syst.* III. 1. *p.* 158. *Enc Méth.* 9. 488. (Satyrus C.)

HABITAT. "India," *Fabricius.* Brazil, (*Enc. Méth.*)

NYMPHALIS LIRISSA.

Pl. XXXVII. fig. 5.

SPECIES. NYMPHALIS LIRISSA: alis subdentatis, cinereis, fusco undatis; anticis fascia alba; posticis punctis quatuor ocellaribus albis. Expans. alar. unc. 1¾.

NYMPHALIS: with the wings slightly dentated, cinereous, with brown waves; the anterior with a white bar, and the posterior with four white eyelets. Expanse of the wings, 1¾ inch.

SYN. Nymphalis Lirissa, *Enc. Méth.* 9. 406.
Papilio (S.) Liria, *Fabr. Ent. Syst.* III. 1. *p.* 239, (*nec* Papilio (N.) Liria, *Fabr. Ent. Syst.* III. 1. *p.* 126.)

HABITAT. "In Indiis," (*Fabricius.*) Brazil, (*Enc. Méth.*)

THECLA ISOCRATES.

♀ Pl. XXXVIII. fig. 1.

FAMILY. LYCÆNIDÆ, *Leach, Stephens.*

GENUS. THECLA, *Fabricius.* (*Syst. Gloss.*) Polyommatus p. *Latreille, Godart.* Cupido p. *Schrank.*

1. Thecla Isocrates. 2. Thecla Pindarus.
3. Thecla Vulcanus.

SPECIES. THECLA ISOCRATES: alis supra fuscis, (♂ cæruleo-micantibus, ♀ macula fulva); posticis (♀) macula submarginali; subtus cinereis, litura gemina strigaque duplici nigricantibus, anguloque ani ocellis duobus. Expanse alar. unc. $1\frac{3}{4}$.

THECLA: with the wings above brown, in the male shining blue, in the female with a fulvous patch; the posterior in the female with a submarginal eyelet; beneath cinereous, with a double mark and double streak of blackish, the anal angle with two eyelets. Expanse of the wings, $1\frac{3}{4}$ inch.

SYN. Papilio (H. R.) Isocrates, *Fabr. Ent. Syst.* III. 1. *p.* 266. *Enc. Méth.* 9. 633.
Papilio (H. R.) Pann, *Fabr. Ent. Syst.* III. 1. *p.* 276. *Donovan,* 1*st edit.* (*nec* Thecla Pan,) *Drury,* 2. *pl.* 23, *fig.* 3, 4.

HABITAT. India, (*Fabricius*). Bengal, (*Enc. Méth.* 9.)

THECLA PINDARUS.

Plate XXXVIII. fig. 2.

SPECIES. THECLA PINDARUS: alis subtricaudatis, supra cæruleis, limbo atro; subtus fuscis argenteo fulvoque maculatis. Expans. alar. unc. $1\frac{1}{2}$.

THECLA: with three short tails; wings above blue with a black border, beneath varied with silvery and fulvous bars. Expanse of the wings, $1\frac{1}{2}$ inch.

SYN. Hesperia (R.) Pindarus, *Fabr. Ent. Syst.* III. 1, *p.* 262.
Polyommatus Vulcanus (var. ♂) *Enc. Méth.* 9. 644.

Donovan observes that " Fabricius describes this beautiful insect as a native of India, and for its figure refers only to the original drawings of W. Jones, Esq. We have ascertained the species from those drawings, collated with the manuscript in the hand-writing of Fabricius, and on this authority give it a place in our selection of Indian insects."

I have hesitated in adopting the opinion of the editors of the Encyclopédie Méthodique, that this is an extraordinary variety of Thecla Vulcanus.

THECLA VULCANUS.

Plate XXXVIII. fig. 3.

SUBGENUS. AMBLYPODIA, *Horsfield.*

SPECIES. THECLA (A.) VULCANUS: alis bicaudatis, supra fuscis; anticis fasciis quatuor, posticis margine fulvis, subtus strigis fulvis argenteisque variegatis. Expans. alar. unc. $1\frac{1}{4}$.

THECLA (A.): with the wings with two tails, above brown; the anterior with four short unequal transverse waved bars, and the posterior with the margin fulvous, beneath varied with fulvous and silvery bars. Expanse of the wings, $1\frac{1}{4}$ inch.

SYN. Hesperia (R.) Vulcanus, *Fabr. Ent. Syst.* III. 1. *p.* 264. *Enc. Méth.* 9. 644. Polyommatus V. ♀. *Horsfield Lep. Jav. p.* 106, (Amblypodia V.)
Papilio Etolus, *Cramer, pl.* 208, *f. E, F.*

Donovan states that the accompanying figures represent the male insect, the female being rather larger, with the colours on the underside more obscure, and the silvery stripes broader. The authors of the Encyclopédie Méthodique describe the male as possessing a shining violet tinge on the upper side, whence the accompanying figures must be females, and the supposed female rather a dark variety of their sex.

THECLA CHITON.

Plate XXXIX. fig. 1.

SPECIES. THECLA CHITON: alis cæruleis, limbo fusco; posticis tricaudatis, (interno parvo) striga marginali alba; subtus flavescenti-albis, nigroque fasciatis. Expans. alar. $1\frac{2}{3}$ unc.

THECLA: with the wings blue, with a black border; the posterior with three tails, (the interior very short, and with a submarginal white line; beneath yellowish white, with black bars. Expanse of the wings, $1\frac{2}{3}$ inch.

SYN. Hesperia (R.) Chiton, *Fabr. Ent. Syst.* III. 1. *p.* 262.
Papilio Silenus, *Cramer Ins. t.* 282 *f. C, D.*
Papilio Agis, *Drury,* 1*st edit. vol.* 3, *pl.* 26, *f.* 3, 4.
Papilio (Pl. Urb.) Phaleros? *Linn. Syst. Nat.* 2. 796. *Enc. Méth.* 9. 629, (Polyommatus Ph.)

HABITAT. India, (*Linnæus, Fabricius*). Brazil, (*Drury*). Surinam, (*Enc. Méth.*)

In the Encyclopédie Méthodique this figure, and that of Drury, (*vol.* 3, *pl.* 26.) are considered as the Papilio Phaleros of Linnæus. The insect here represented is a male, according to the distinctions given in the Encyclopédie, but it has not the large orbicular brown spot near the middle of the anterior wings, so that it is, perhaps, doubtful whether the P. Phaleros, *Linnæus,* and the P. Chiton, *Fabricius,* be really identical, as Donovan had suggested.

THECLA HERODOTUS.

Plate XXXIX. fig. 2.

SPECIES. THECLA HERODOTUS: alis caudatis, cæruleis, subtus viridibus; posticis striga submarginali punctorum, extus alborum et intus nigrorum. Expans. alar. $1\frac{1}{6}$ unc.

Pl. XXXIX

1. Thecla Chiton. 2. Th. Herodotus. 3. Th. Pythagoras.
4. Polyommatus Florus.

LEPIDOPTERA.

THECLA: with the wings tailed, above blue, beneath green; the posterior pair with a submarginal row of dots, white without and black within. Expanse of the wings, 1⅙ inch.

SYN. Hesperia (R.) Herodotus, *Fabr. Ent. Syst.* III. 1. *p.* 286. *Enc. Méth.* 9. 641, (Polyommatus H.)
Papilio Amyntor, *Cramer, pl.* 48, *fig. E.*
♀ Papilio Eryx, *Linn. Mantissa,* 1. 537. *Fabr. Ent. Syst.* III, 1. *p.* 283.
Papilio Menalcas, *Cramer, pl.* 259, *fig. A, B.*

HABITAT. "In Indiis," (*Fabricius*). Surinam, (*Enc. Meth.*)

THECLA PYTHAGORAS.

Plate XXXIX. fig. 3.

SPECIES. THECLA PYTHAGORAS: alis tricaudatis, atris, disco fulvo, lunulisque submarginalibus; posticarum fulvis; subtus nigris albo variis fasciaque media alba, punctisque duobus irroratis ad angulum ani. Expans. alar. unc. 1⅙.

THECLA: with the wings three-tailed, black, with the disc of each fulvous; the posterior with submarginal fulvous spots; beneath black varied with white, with a white central bar, and with two eyes at the anal angle. Expanse of the wings, 1⅙ inch.

SYN. Hesperia (R.) Pythagoras, *Fabr. Ent. Syst.* III. 1, *p.* 259. *Enc. Meth.* 9. 619, (Polyommatus P.)
Var. (caudis mutilis) Hesperia (R.) Juba, *Fabr. Ent. Syst.* III. 1. *p.* 314.

Fabricius states the habitat of Pythagoras to be "In Indiis," but that of Juba, which is a variety of the same species, with the tails broken off, to be Sierra Leone. In the Encyclopédie Méthodique, the western coast of Africa is given as the habitat of Pythagoras.

POLYOMMATUS FLORUS.

Plate XXXIX. fig. 4.

GENUS. POLYOMMATUS, *Latreille.*

SPECIES. POLYOMMATUS FLORUS: alis integerrimis, fulvis, margine nigro; anticis supra punctis duobus; subtus omnibus basi punctis plurimis nigris. Expans. alar. unc. 1.

POLYOMMATUS: with the wings entire, fulvous, with a slender black margin; the anterior above with two black spots; beneath all the wings at the base spotted with black. Expanse of the wings, 1 inch.

SYN. Hesperia (R). Florus, *Fabr. Ent. Syst.* III. 1, *p.* 310.

HABITAT. "In Indiis," (*Fabricius*).

THECLA LISIAS.

Plate XL. fig. 1.

SPECIES. THECLA LISIAS: alis tricaudatis; anticis fuscis macula magna fulva; posticis supra fuscis, margineque postico cæruleo maculato; subtus albis nigro-maculatis. Expans. alar. unc. 1¼.

THECLA: with three tails; the anterior wings brown, with a large fulvous spot; the posterior above brown, with the posterior margin spotted with blue; beneath white with black marks. Expanse of the wings, 1¼ inch.

SYN. Hesperia (R.) Lisias, *Fabr. Ent. Syst.* III. 1, *p.* 261.

HABITAT. "Poulicandor, *Mus. Dom. Banks*," (*Fabricius*).

THECLA SOPHOCLES.

Plate XL. fig. 2.

SPECIES. THECLA SOPHOCLES: alis bicaudatis, nigris, disco communi cæruleo; subtus albis, strigis undatis flavescentibus; posticis puncto anali fulvo. Expans. alar. unc. 1½.

THECLA: with two tails, black, with the disc blue; beneath white with several waved yellowish lines; the posterior pair with an anal fulvous eyelet. Expanse of the wings, 1½ inch.

SYN. Hesperia (R.) Sophocles, *Fabr. Ent. Syst.* III. 1, *p.* 267. *Enc. Méth.* 9. 631, (Polyommatus S.)

HABITAT. "In Indiis," (*Fabricius*).

THECLA JARBAS.

Plate XL. fig. 3.

SPECIES. THECLA JARBAS: alis caudatis, fulvis, limbo fusco; subtus cinereis striga alba; posticis punctis duobus atris. Expans. alar. unc. 1½.

THECLA: with the wings tailed, fulvous, with the border brown; beneath cinereous with a white bar; the posterior pair with two black spots. Expanse of the wings, 1½ inch.

SYN. Hesperia (R.) Jarbas, *Fabr. Ent. Syst.* III. 1, *p.* 276. *Enc. Méth.* 9. 646. *Horsfield Lep. Jav. p.* 93, (Thecla J.)

HABITAT. "Siam, *Mus. Dom. Banks*," (*Fabricius*). Bengal and Java, (*Enc. Méth.*)

1. Thecla Lisias. 2. Thecla Sophocles.
3. Thecla Jarbas. 4. Thecla Thäles.

PL. XLI

1. Thecla. Melibœus 2. Th. Tyrtæus. 3. Th. Xenophon.

4. Th. Achæus. 5. Th. Phorbas.

LEPIDOPTERA.

THECLA THALES.

Plate XL. fig. 4.

SPECIES. THECLA THALES: alis bicaudatis, utrinque atris, subtus lunulis cæruleis; posticis fascia submarginali aurea. Expans. alar. unc. $1\frac{1}{4}$.

THECLA: with two tails, the wings on both sides black, beneath with blue lunules; the posterior also with an abbreviated submarginal golden fascia. Expanse of the wings, $1\frac{1}{4}$ inch.

SYN. Hesperia (R.) Thales, *Fabricius Ent. Syst.* III. 1, *p.* 268. *Enc. Méth.* 9. 625; (Polyommatus T.)

HABITAT. "In Indiis, (*Fabricius*). Brazil, (*Enc. Méth.*)

THECLA MELIBŒUS.

Plate XLI. fig. 1.

SPECIES. THECLA MELIBŒUS: alis bicaudatis, cærulescentibus, limbo fusco; subtus flavescentibus; anticis fusco, posticis nigro strigosis, angulo ani atro; annulis cæruleis. Expans. alar. unc. $1\frac{1}{3}$.

THECLA: with two tails, the wings blue above with a brown border; beneath yellowish, the anterior with brown and the posterior with black streaks; anal angle black with two blue rings. Expanse of the wings, $1\frac{1}{3}$ inch.

SYN. Hesperia (R.) Melibœus, *Fabr. Ent. Syst.* III. 1. *p.* 271. *Enc. Méth.* 9. 629, (Polyommatus M.)

HABITAT. "In India, (*Fabricius*). Brazil, (*Enc. Méth.*)

THECLA TYRTÆUS.

Plate XLI. fig. 2.

SPECIES. THECLA TYRTÆUS: alis bicaudatis, fuscis; posticis subtus striga undata alba lunulisque submarginalibus nigris, intermediis rufis. Expans. alar. unc. 1.

THECLA: with two tails, wings above brown; beneath the posterior have a waved white streak and black submarginal lunules, the two middle lunules being red. Expanse of the wings, 1 inch.

SYN. Hesperia (R.) Tyrtæus, *Fabr. Ent. Syst.* III. 1. *p.* 271. *Enc. Méth.* 9. 637, (Polyommatus T.)

HABITAT. "In India," (*Fabricius*).

THECLA XENOPHON.

Plate XLI. fig. 3.

SPECIES. THECLA XENOPHON: alis bicaudatis fuscis, disco flavo; subtus cinereo, striga media alba fusco strigaque innata; posticarum marginali fusca. Expans. alar. unc. $1\frac{1}{8}$.

THECLA: with two tails, wings brown, with a yellow disc, beneath cinereous, with a central white and brown streak; the posterior also with a brown submarginal line. Expanse of the wings, $1\frac{1}{8}$ inch.

SYN. Hesperia (R.) Xenophon, *Fabr. Ent. Syst.* III. 1. *p.* 272. *Enc. Méth.* 9. 640. (Polyommatus X.) *Horsfield Lep. Jav. p.* 93, *pl.* 4, *f.* 2, 2*a*, (larva et pupa).

Papilio Melampus, *Cramer, pl.* 362, *f. G, H.*

HABITAT. "In India," (*Fabricius*). Java, (*Horsfield*).

Dr. Horsfield has traced the metamorphoses of this species, and pointed out the distinction between it and Jarbas, plate XL. fig. 3. The caterpillar is more elongate than the ordinaryonisciform larvæ, with short stumps of fascicles. It varies in colour from yellow, with a greenish cast, to a dark ferruginous brown, with lateral bands. It feeds upon Schmiedelia racemosa, and was found in considerable abundance by Dr. Horsfield in Java.

THECLA ACHÆUS.

Plate XLI. fig. 4.

SPECIES. THECLA ACHÆUS: alis subbicaudatis fuscis; maculis flavis; subtus flavis maculis aureis, numerosis, quibusdem fusco-cinctis. Expans. alar. unc. $1\frac{3}{4}$.

THECLA: with two short tails, wings brown, above with yellow spots; beneath pale yellow, with numerous golden spots, some of which are edged with purplish brown. Expanse of the wings, $1\frac{3}{4}$ inch.

SYN. Hesperia (R.) Achæus, *Fabr. Ent. Syst.* III. 1. *p.* 273. *Cramer Pap. pl.* 352, *f. G, H. Enc. Méth.* 9. 644, (Polyommatus A.)

HABITAT. "In India," (*Fabricius*). Surinam, (*Enc. Méth.*)

PL XLII.

1. Thecla Æolus. 2. Thecla Strephon.

3. Thecla Philippus 4. Thecla Pericles.

LEPIDOPTERA.

THECLA PHORBAS.

Plate XLI. fig. 5.

SPECIES. THECLA PHORBAS: alis caudatis, fuscis, disco albo; subtus albis, cinereo strigosis, punctis duobus anguli ani atris. Expans. alar. unc. 1⅗.

THECLA: with the wings tailed, brown, with a white disc; beneath white with ash-coloured streaks, and with two small black eyes at the anal angle. Expanse of the wings, 1⅗ inch.

SYN. Hesperia (R.) Phorbas, *Fab. Ent. Syst.* III. 1. *p.* 277. *Enc. Méth.* 9. 646, (Polyommatus P.)

HABITAT. "In India," (*Fabricius*).

THECLA ÆOLUS. ♂

Plate XLII. fig. 1.

SPECIES. THECLA ÆOLUS: alis caudatis, cyaneis, nitidis, margine fusco, macula nigra; subtus fuscis, fascia communi alba nigroque striata. Expans. alar. unc. 1¾.

THECLA: with the wings tailed, above blue in the disc, shining, with a brown margin and a black central spot; beneath brown, with a common white band, and with black streaks. Expanse of the wings, 1¾ inch.

SYN. Hesperia Æolus, *Fabr. Ent. Syst.* III. 1. *p.* 284. *Enc. Méth.* 9. 628, (Polyommatus Æ.)

Papilio Thallus, *Cramer Pap. pl.* 259, *f. C, D.*

♀ Hesperia Pelion, *Fabr. Ent. Syst.* III. 1. *p.* 213. *Cramer, pl.* 6, *f. E, F.*

HABITAT. "In Indiis," (*Fabricius*). Guiana, (*Enc. Méth.*)

THECLA STREPHON.

Plate XLII. fig. 2.

SPECIES. THECLA STREPHON: alis caudatis, fuscis; disco cærulescentibus; subtus cinereis fascia alba, anguloque ani ocello gemino rufo pupilla nigra. Expans. alar. unc. 1½.

THECLA: with the wings tailed, brown; the disc bluish; beneath cinereous with a white fascia, and with a double red ocellus, having a black pupil, at the anal angle. Expanse of the wings, 1½ inch.

SYN. Hesperia (R.) Strephon, *Fab. Ent. Syst.* III. 1. *p.* 281. *Enc. Méth.* 9. 632? (Polyommatus S.)

Papilio Cyllarus, *Cramer Pap. pl.* 27, *fig. C, D.*

HABITAT. "In India orientali," (*Fabricius*). Surinam, and Brazil, (*Enc. Méth.*)

THECLA PHILIPPUS.

Plate XLII. fig. 3.

SPECIES. THECLA PHILIPPUS: alis caudatis, fuscis; subtus albis; posticis supra striga postica alba punctisque duobus subocellaribus anguli ani atris. Expans. alar. unc. $1\frac{1}{4}$.

THECLA: with the wings tailed, brown; beneath white; the posterior above with a posterior white streak, and two eyelets at the anal angle of a black colour. Expanse of the wings, $1\frac{1}{4}$ inch.

SYN. Hesperia R. Philippus, *Fabr. Ent. Syst.* III. 1. *p.* 283. *Enc. Méth.* 9. 646, (Polyommatus P.)

HABITAT. "In India," (*Fabricius*).

THECLA PERICLES.

Plate XLII. fig. 4.

SPECIES. THECLA PERICLES: alis bicaudatis, nigris, immaculatis; subtus fuscis albo undatis; posticis angulo ani macula duplici argentea, punctisque aliquot nigris. Expans. alar. unc. $1\frac{1}{4}$.

THECLA: with two tails, wings black, immaculate; beneath brown with white waved lines; posterior with a double silvery spot at the anal angle, and with several black points. Expanse of the wings, $1\frac{1}{4}$ inch.

SYN. Hesperia (R.) Pericles, *Fabr. Ent. Syst.* III. 1. *p.* 273. *Enc Méth.* 9. 622, (Polyommatus P.)

HABITAT. "In Indiis," (*Fabricius*).

ERYCINA THUCYDIDES.

Plate XLIII. fig. 1.

SPECIES. ERYCINA THUCYDIDES: alis integerrimis, nigris; macula magna media fulva in singula; subtus cinereis rufo undatis. Expans. alar. unc. $1\frac{1}{2}$.

ERYCINA: with the wings entire, black, with a large fulvous spot in the centre of each; beneath cinereous with red wavy lines. Expanse of the wings, $1\frac{1}{2}$ inch.

SYN. Hesperia (R) Thucydides, *Fabr. Ent. Syst.* III. 1. *p.* 323. *Enc. Méth.* 9. 589, (Erycina T.)

HABITAT. "In Indiis," (*Fabricius.*)

PL. XLIII

1. Erycina Thucidides. 2. Erycina Petronius.

3. Er. Regulus. 4 Er. Lucanus.

LEPIDOPTERA.

ERYCINA PETRONIUS.

Plate XLIII. fig. 2.

SPECIES. ERYCINA PETRONIUS: alis integris cæruleis, strigis apiceque nigris; subtus fusco-cinereis, nigro punctatis. Expans. alar. unc. $1\frac{3}{4}$.

ERYCINA: with the wings entire, blue, with black streaks and posterior margins; beneath brownish ashy, with black spots. Expanse of the wings, $1\frac{3}{4}$ inch.

SYN. Hesperia (R.) Petronius, *Fabr. Ent. Syst.* III. 1. *p.* 324. *Enc. Méth.* 9. 570, (Erycina P.)

♀ Papilio Menander, *Cramer Pap. tab.* 334, *f. C, D.*

HABITAT. "In Indiis," (*Fabricius*). Guiana and Brazil, (*Enc. Méth.*)

ERYCINA REGULUS.

Plate XLIII. fig. 3.

SPECIES. ERYCINA REGULUS: alis integerrimis, nigris, fasciis duabus albis aut flavescentibus, externa anticarum interrupta. Expans. alar. unc. $1\frac{1}{3}$.

ERYCINA: with the wings entire, black, with two white or yellowish broad bands, the outer in the anterior wings being broken. Expanse of the wings, $1\frac{1}{3}$ inch.

SYN. Hesperia (R.) Regulus, *Fabr. Ent. Syst.* III. 1. *p.* 318. *Enc. Méth.* 9. 589. (Erycina R.)

HABITAT. "In Indiis," (*Fabricius*). Brazil, (*Enc. Méth.*)

ERYCINA LUCANUS.

Plate XLIII. fig. 4.

SPECIES. ERYCINA LUCANUS: alis integerrimis, supra flavis, macula media anticarum limboque omni nigris; subtus anticis flavescentibus fusco-maculatis; posticis rubris flavo irroratis et fusco-maculatis. Expans. alar. unc. $1\frac{1}{4}$.

ERYCINA: with the wings entire, above yellow, with a central spot in the anterior pair and all the edges black; beneath the anterior yellowish, with brown spots; the posterior red, with yellow dots and brown spots. Expanse of the wings, $1\frac{1}{4}$ inch.

SYN. Hesperia (R.) Lucanus, *Fabr. Syst. Ent.* III. 1. *p.* 322. *Enc. Méth.* 9. 586, (Erycina L.)

HABITAT. "In Indiis," (*Fabricius*).

The accompanying figure of a species described by Fabricius, from the collection of Drury, and the drawings of Mr. Jones, (from which also Donovan, in all probability, obtained his acquaintance with the species,) enables us to clear up the confusion in the

Fabrician description, in which the wings are described—" *supra* flavæ macula media anticarum, *disco* que omni nigris"; the description in the short specific character being " alis nigris, *disco* flavo." Hence it is evident that, in the former description, the term " disco" was accidentally used instead of " limbo." In the Encyclopédie Méthodique the confusion is increased, by the employment of the word " dessous," instead of " dessus."*

ERYCINA TARQUINIUS.

Plate XLIV. fig. 1.

SPECIES. ERYCINA TARQUINIUS: alis integris, nigris; anticis macula oblonga baseos sinuata postice triloba; posticis angulo anali late flavo punctis quinque nigris; subtus cinereis maculis nigris et rufescentibus, his albo cinctis. Expans. alar. unc. $1\frac{1}{3}$.

ERYCINA: with the wings entire, black; the anterior with an oblong sinuated spot at the base, the extremity of which is trilobed; the posterior with a broad yellow patch at the anal angle, having five black dots; beneath cinereous, with black and red spots, the latter encircled with white. Expanse of the wings, $1\frac{1}{3}$ inch.

SYN. Hesperia (R.) Tarquinius, *Fabr. Ent. Syst.* III. 1. *p.* 319. *Enc Méth.* 9. 580, (Erycina T.)

HABITAT. " In Indiis," (*Fabricius*).

ERYCINA ÆMULIUS.

Plate XLIV. fig. 2.

SPECIES. ERYCINA ÆMULIUS: alis integris, cinereis, lineolis transversis albidis maculisque oblongis fuscis; posticis supra pallidis; subtus omnibus maculis plurimis fuscis. Expans. alar. unc. $1\frac{1}{4}$.

ERYCINA: with the wings entire, cinereous, with short transverse whitish lines and oblong brown spots; the posterior pair above pale; the under surface of all the wings much spotted with brown. Expanse of the wings, $1\frac{1}{4}$ inch.

SYN. Hesperia (R.) Æmulius, *Fabr. Ent. Syst.* III. 1. *p.* 322. *Enc. Méth.* 9. 580, (Erycina Æ.)

* In the first edition of this work, Erycina Salustius was introduced in the text, after the foregoing species; but no figure of it appeared in the plates, I have therefore omitted it.—(T. O. W.)

PL. XLIV

1. Erycina Tarquinius. 2. Erycina Æmulius.

3. Hesperia Numitor.

PL. XLV.

1. Polyommatus Plinius. 2. P. Plato. 3. P. Hippocrates.
4. Thecla Theocritus 5. P. Parrhasius.

LEPIDOPTERA.

HESPERIA NUMITOR.

Plate XLIV. fig. 3.

FAMILY. HESPERIIDÆ, *Stephens.*

GENUS. HESPERIA, *Latreille, Godart.* Battus p. *Scop.* Papilio (Pl. Rur.) *Linnæus.*

SPECIES. HESPERIA NUMITOR: alis integerrimis, fuscis; posticis supra disco flavo; subtus flavis, anticis disco fusco. Expans. alar. unc. 1—1¼.

HESPERIA: with the wings entire, brown; the posterior with the disc above yellow; the under surface of all the wings yellow, except the disc of the anterior, which is brown. Expanse of the wings, 1 to 1¼ inch.

SYN. Hesperia (R.) Numitor, *Fabr. Ent. Syst.* III. 1. *p.* 324. *Enc. Méth.* 9. 777.

HABITAT. "In Indiis," (*Fabricius*). Philadelphia, (*Enc. Méth.*)

Donovan has evidently introduced this, as well as many of the preceding butterflies, (especially those belonging to the great genus Erycina, which are almost exclusively Brazilian,) into the present work, on the authority of the loose habitat of Fabricius, "In Indiis." The Hesperia Numitor is, however, an inhabitant of North America, having been sent from Philadelphia to M. Latreille by M. Lesueur. I have also received it from the same city, in a large collection of insects of that country, for which I am indebted to the liberality of Mr. Titian R. Peale, the curator of the Museum of Philadelphia, a very zealous entomologist.

POLYOMMATUS PLINIUS.

Plate XLV. fig. 1.

SPECIES. POLYOMMATUS PLINIUS: alis caudatis, albo nigroque variis; anticis supra maculis quadratis fuscis; omnibus subtus albis, fusco et nigro transverse strigosis, serie duplici punctorum submarginalium punctoque gemmo aureo ad angulum ani posticarum. Expans. alar. unc. 1.

POLYOMMATUS: with the wings tailed, and varied above with black and white; the anterior above with square brown spots; all the wings beneath white, with transverse brown or black streaks, and with a double row of submarginal dots; the posterior with a double golden spot at the anal angle. Expanse of the wings, 1 inch.

SYN. Hesperia (R.) Plinius, *Fabr. Ent. Syst.* III. 1. *p.* 284. *Enc. Méth.* 9. 658, (Polyommatus Pl.) *Horsfield Lep. Jav.* 1. *p.* 72.

POLYOMMATUS PLATO.

Plate XLV. fig. 2.

SPECIES. POLYOMMATUS PLATO: alis caudatis, supra cæruleis limbo fusco; posticis punctis marginalibus atris; subtus cinereis albo undatis, posticis ocello atro iride flava, pupillaque duplici argentea et ad angulum ani macula argentea. Expans. alar. unc. $1\frac{1}{4}$.

POLYOMMATUS: with the wings tailed; above blue with a brown border; the posterior with marginal black dots; beneath cinereous with white waves, the posterior with a black ocellus, having the iris yellow, and a double silvery pupil, a silvery spot also at the anal angle. Expanse of the wings, $1\frac{1}{4}$ inch.

SYN. Hesperia (R.) Plato, *Fab. Ent. Syst.* III. 1. *p.* 288?
Polyommatus Plato, *Enc. Méth.* 9. 655?

HABITAT. "In Indiis," (*Fabricius*).

The description of the ocelli on the under side of the under wings of the insect described under this name, not agreeing with the Fabrician description, I have given the quotation with a mark of doubt.

POLYOMMATUS HIPPOCRATES.

Plate XLV. fig. 3.

SPECIES. POLYOMMATUS HIPPOCRATES: alis caudatis; supra fuscis, anticis apice, posticis margine tenui albis; subtus albidis, anticis striga punctorum, posticis punctis sparsis, nigris. Expans. alar. unc. 1.

POLYOMMATUS: with the wings tailed; above brown, the tips of the anterior and a slender margin to the posterior white; beneath whitish, the anterior with a row of black spots, and the latter with several irregularly placed black spots. Expanse of the wings, 1 inch.

SYN. Hesperia (R.) Hippocrates, *Fabr. Ent. Syst.* III. 1, *p.* 288. *Enc. Méth.* 9. 659, (Polyommatus H.)

THECLA THEOCRITUS.

Plate XLV. fig. 4.

SPECIES. THECLA THEOCRITUS; alis caudatis; supra virescentibus aureo nitidulis, costa lata obscuriore; subtus nigris, strigis aliquot e punctis parvis flavescentibus. Expans. alar. unc. $1\frac{1}{2}$.

LEPIDOPTERA.

THECLA: with the wings tailed; above greenish with golden spangles, and with the front margin and tip dark; beneath black, with several rows of small yellowish dots. Expanse of the wings, $1\frac{1}{2}$ inch.

SYN. Hesperia (R.) Theocritus, *Fabr. Ent. Syst.* III. 1. *p.* 289. *Enc. Méth.* 9. 653, (Polyommatus Th.)

POLYOMMATUS PARRHASIUS.

Plate XLV. fig. 5.

SPECIES. POLYOMMATUS PARRHASIUS: alis caudatis; supra cæruleis margine fusco, (♂), aut fuscis, (♀); posticis ante marginem striga punctorum nigrorum ocellatorum; omnibus subtus cinereis, pone medium albo undatis; posticis punctis tribus baseos atris, albo cinctis, apiceque punctis quatuor aureis, tertio puncto atro. Expans. alar. $\frac{3}{4}$—1 unc.

POLYOMMATUS: with the wings tailed; above blue with a brown margin in the male, brown in the female, the posterior with a submarginal row of black ocellated spots; the under side of all the wings cinereous, with white waves beyond the middle, the posterior with three black spots, edged with white towards the base, and with four golden marginal spots, the third having a black dot in the middle. Expanse of the wings, $\frac{3}{4}$ to 1 inch.

SYN. Hesperia (R.) Parrhasius, *Fabr. Ent. Syst.* III. 1. *p.* 289. *Enc. Méth.* 9. 657, (Polyommatus P.) *Horsfield Lep. Jav.* 1. *p.* 86?

HABITAT. "In India," (*Fabricius, Enc. Méth.*) Java, (*Horsfield*).

As in our little English "blues," (as the species of Polyommatus are called by collectors,) there are many species so very closely allied together, that it is very difficult to settle their specific distinctions, so there appear to be several Indian species so nearly related to Pol. Parrhasius, that it is only by precisely following the particular description of that species given by Fabricius, (and which I have embodied in the above definition,) that we can avoid confusion. The species was known to Fabricius, through the drawings of Mr. Jones, and the collection of Mr. Drury, to both of which Donovan had access, so that we may adopt his figures as the real representatives of the Fabrician insect. It is on these grounds that I have attached a mark of doubt to the reference to Dr. Horsfield's Lepidoptera Javanica. Donovan has, however, fallen into the strange mistake of considering the larger individual with blue wings as the female, and the smaller brown one as the male, whereas, as in the common English "blues," the opposite is the case.

ERYCINA? BIBULUS.

Plate XLVI. fig. 1.

SPECIES. ERYCINA? BIBULUS: alis integerrimis; supra fuscis, anticis in medio litura cinerea; subtus anticis cinereis punctis aliquot apicis fuscis annulo argenteo cinctis, strigaque marginali argentea; posticis albis striga media argentea, punctis aliquot fuscis apice fusco punctis argenteis. Expans. alar. unc. $1\frac{1}{4}$.

ERYCINA? with the wings entire; above brown, the anterior with a cinereous stripe in the centre; beneath the anterior cinereous, with several apical brown spots surrounded with silver, and a marginal silver stripe; posterior white, with a central silver bar, several brown spots, and the apex brown with silvery spots. Expanse of the wings, $1\frac{1}{4}$ inch.

SYN. Hesperia (R.) Bibulus, *Fabr. Ent. Syst.* III. 1. *p.* 307.

HABITAT. "In Indiis," (*Fabricius*).

POLYOMMATUS HYLAX.

Plate XLVI. fig. 2.

SPECIES. POLYOMMATUS HYLAX: alis integris, supra fuscis immaculatis, subtus cinereis, punctis nigris arcubus submarginalibus fuscis. Expans. alar. $\frac{5}{6}$ unc.

POLYOMMATUS: with the wings entire, brown above without spots, beneath cinereous with black spots, and with a row of submarginal lunules, (behind which is a row of small black dots). Expanse of the wings, $\frac{5}{6}$ of an inch.

SYN. Hesperia (R.) Hylax, *Fabr. Mant. Ins.* 2. *p.* 77. *Ent. Syst.* III. 1. *p.* 304. *Enc. Méth.* 9. 701, (Polyommatus H.) *nec* Pithecops Hylax, *Horsfield Lep. Jav.* 1, *p.* 66, *pl.* 1, *f.* 2, 2 *a.*

Papilio Lysimon, *Ochsenheimer Pap. Eur. t.* 1? *Enc. Méth.* 9. 701?

HABITAT. "In India orientali," (*Fabricius*).

I can by no means agree with Dr. Horsfield, in considering the insect which he has figured under the name of Pithecops Hylax as identical with the Fabrician insect, as that which is here figured is marked more agreeably with the original description of the species, short as it is. Had Fabricius been describing Dr. Horsfield's insect, he would have said "strigis duabus submarginalibus punctorum nigrorum," instead of "nigropunctatis," which implies a general scattering of dots over the wings; moreover Dr. Horsfield's insect exhibits no trace of the "arcubus fuscis," described by Fabricius.

PL. XLVI

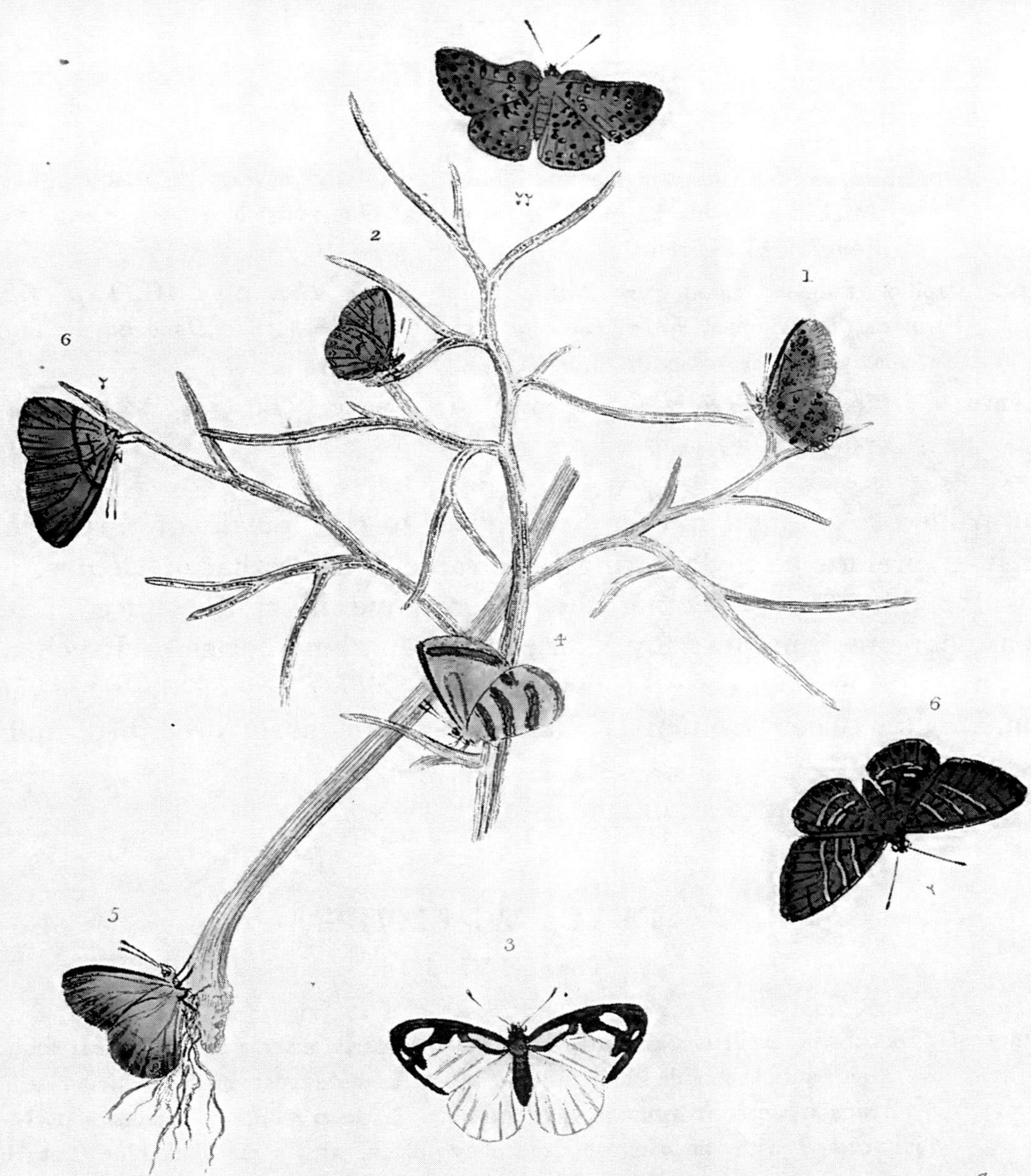

1. Erycina? Bibulus. 2. Polyommatus Hylax. 3. Erycina Athemon,
4. E? Livius 5. Thecla Romulus. 6. E. Ptolomaeus 7. E. Ovidius

LEPIDOPTERA.

ERYCINA ATHEMON. ♂.

Plate XLVI. fig. 3.

SPECIES. ERYCINA ATHEMON: alis integris, albis; anticis margine exteriori nigro, cæruleo alboque maculato. Expans. alar. 1—1½ unc.

ERYCINA: with the wings entire, white; the anterior having the front margin broadly marked with black, in which are several blue and white spots. Expanse of the wings, 1 to 1½ inch.

SYN. Papilio Athemon, *Linn. Syst. Nat.* 2. 792. *Fabr. Ent. Syst.* III. 1, *p.* 318, (♀).
Hesperia (R.) Cœnus, *Fabr. Ent. Syst.* III. 1. *p.* 308. (♂). *Donovan*, 1*st edit.*
Erycina Arthemom, *Enc. Méth.* 9. 578.

HABITAT. "In Indiis," (*Fabricius*, Cœnus). In America, (*Linnæus*, Athemom). Brazil, (*Enc. Méth.*)

The name of Athemon having been given to the female of this species, I have adopted it in preference to following Donovan and using that of Cœnus, proposed by Fabricius for the male, rejecting the latter name in consequence of its similarity to Ceneus, a name employed by Fabricius for another species of Erycina. It is customary, however, in such cases, to adopt the specific name of the male rather than of the female, where they happen to have been previously described under different names.

ERYCINA? LIVIUS.

Plate XLVI. fig. 4.

SPECIES. ERYCINA? LIVIUS: alis integerrimis; supra atris, macula disci cærulea; subtus cinereis; anticis macula oblonga baseos flava, argenteo marginata; posticis fasciis tribus rufis argenteo marginatis, margine flavo, fascia argentea. Expans. alar. 1⅙ unc.

ERYCINA? with the wings entire; above black, with a discoidal blue spot; beneath cinereous; the anterior with an oblong basal yellow spot, margined with silver; the apex yellow, with a broad brown bar, margined with silver; the posterior with three red bars margined with silver, the margins yellow with a silver line. Expanse of the wings, 1⅙ inch.

SYN. Hesperia (R.) Livius, *Fabr. Ent. Syst* III. 1. *p.* 315. *Enc. Méth.* 9. 825, (Nymphalis L.)

HABITAT. "In Indiis," (*Fabricius*).

THECLA ROMULUS.

Plate XLVI. fig. 5.

SPECIES. THECLA ROMULUS: alis integerrimis; supra fuscis, immaculatis; subtus viridibus, anticis immaculatis, posticis striga fusca, maculaque postica rufa. Expans. alar. unc. $1\frac{1}{6}$.

THECLA: with the wings entire; above brown, immaculate; beneath green, the anterior without spots, the posterior with a brown stripe, and a submarginal red ocellus. Expanse of the wings, $1\frac{1}{6}$ inch.

SYN. Hesperia (R.) Romulus, *Fabr. Ent. Syst.* III. 1. *p.* 316. *Enc. Méth.* 9. 674. (Polyommatus R.)

HABITAT. "In Indiis," (*Fabricius*).

The accompanying figure exhibits no trace of the brown line on the under surface of the posterior wings described by Fabricius, from the drawings of Mr. Jones, and the collection of Drury.

ERYCINA PTOLOMÆUS. ♂.

Plate XLVI. fig. 6.

SPECIES. ERYCINA PTOLOMÆUS: alis integerrimis; supra ferrugineis, strigis plurimis fuscis, ultima ante marginem punctata; subtus (mas) cæruleis, (fem.) rufis, basi cærulescente. Expans. alar. unc. $1\frac{1}{2}$ unc.

ERYCINA: with the wings entire; above ferruginous with several brown streaks, the submarginal one being composed of points; beneath in the male blue, in the female ferruginous, with the base paler blue. Expanse of the wings, $1\frac{1}{2}$ inch.

SYN. Hesperia (R.) Ptolomæus, *Fabr. Ent. Syst.* III. 1. *p.* 319, ♂. *Enc. Méth.* 9. 572, (Erycina Pt.)

Hesperia (R.) Lucius, *Fabr. Ent. Syst.* III. 1. *p.* 320, ♀.

HABITAT. "In Indiis," (*Fabricius*). Brazil, (*Enc. Méth.*)

ERYCINA OVIDIUS.

Plate XLVI. fig. 7.

SPECIES. ERYCINA OVIDIUS: alis integris, supra fulvis, subtus flavescentibus; utrinque strigis sex undatis, feminæ nigris, maris aureo pulverulentis. Expans. alar. unc. $1\frac{1}{4}$.

PL. XLVII.

1. Leptocircus Curius. 2. Hesperia Propertius.

3. Hesperia Tibullus.

ERYCINA: with the wings entire, above fulvous, beneath yellowish, on each side with six waved stripes, black in the female, but spotted with gold in the male. Expanse of the wings, $1\frac{1}{4}$ inch.

SYN. Hesperia (R.) Ovidius, *Fabr. Ent. Syst.* III. 1. *p.* 320. *Enc. Méth.* 9. 571.
Papilio Fatima, *Cramer, pl.* 271, *f. A, B,* ♂. *C, D,* ♀.

HABITAT. "In Indiis," (*Fabricius*). East Indies, (*Enc. Meth.*)

The seven preceding species are represented upon the Adiantum succulentum.

LEPTOCIRCUS CURIUS.

Plate XLVII. fig. 1.

FAMILY. PAPILIONIDÆ.

GENUS. LEPTOCIRCUS, *Swainson.* (Lamproptera, *G. R. Gray.* Erycina p. *Enc. Méth.* Iphiclides, *Hubner.*)

SPECIES. LEPTOCIRCUS CURIUS: alis concoloribus, nigris, fascia communi glauca; anticis ante apicem hyalinis. Expans. alar. unc. $1\frac{3}{4}$.

LEPTOCIRCUS: with the wings concolorous, black, with a common greenish white fascia; the anterior having a large transparent spot near the apex. Expanse of the wings, $1\frac{3}{4}$ inches.

SYN. Papilio (Eq. Ach.) Curius, *Fabr. Ent. Syst.* III. 1. *p.* 28. *Enc. Méth.* 9. 564, 827, (Erycina C.)
Leilus [Urania] (Leptocircus) Curius, *Swainson Zool. Illust. 2d series, pl.* 106.
Leptocircus Curius, *Boisduval Hist. Nat. Lepid.* 1. 381, *pl.* 17, *f.* 3. *Naturalist's Library Entomol. vol.* 5, *pl.* 5, *fig.* 1.
Erycina (Lamproptera) Curius, *G. R. Gray in Griff. An. Kingd. Ins. pl.* 102, *f.* 4.

HABITAT. Siam, (*Fabricius*). Java, (*Boisduval*).

This insect is exceedingly interesting, with reference to the general classification of the diurnal butterflies. It was, by Fabricius, regarded as a true Papilio, and certainly the head, palpi, antennæ, legs, &c. clearly prove the correctness of this affinity. In the Encyclopédie Méthodique, however, it was considered as an Erycina, doubtless from its small size, and its apparent resemblance to some of the long-tailed species, such as Rhetus and Dorilas of Cramer. Donovan also asserted its greater affinity to the Papiliones Plebeii. Mr. Swainson next proved it to belong to the family Papilionidæ, by his figures of the various parts in detail; but, from too eagerly following out his peculiar theories, he gave it as a subgenus of the genus Urania, which name he changed to Leilus, (considering its type to be the Papilio Leilus of Linnæus,) on the ground that the name Urania had been employed in Botany, which is certainly the case; but as the genus of plants ought to retain its *previous* name Ravenala, the name of Urania is not inapplicable to a genus of Lepidoptera. But Leptocircus ought clearly not to be regarded as belonging to the same group as Leilus, Orontes, and Rhipheus, together with Patroclus, Lunus, and Empedocles, which decidedly belong thereto, although omitted by Mr. Swainson. The veins of the wings of Leptocircus are decidedly Papilionideous, and have no resemblance whatever to those of Urania. There is it is true some analogy in the *form* of the posterior wings, but, I presume, no real relation can be supported on such a character, and I can discover no other to give it a relation either with Urania, or Erycina. In the male of this insect, the pale band crossing the wings is of a greenish white, but in the female it is transparent white in the anterior, and white in the posterior wings.

The species was described by Fabricius from a specimen in the collection of Sir J. Banks. It is become sufficiently common.

HESPERIA PROPERTIUS.

Plate XLVII. fig. 2.

FAMILY. HESPERIIDÆ.

GENUS. HESPERIA.

SPECIES. HESPERIA PROPERTIUS: alis supra nigris, anticis lineolis duabus marginalibus baseos maculisque flavis, posticis fascia flava; subtus, anticis atro, flavo, rufoque variis, posticis fasciis rufis flavisque margine tenuiori nigro. Expans. alar. unc. $1\frac{1}{2}$.

HESPERIA: with the wings above black, the anterior with two marginal lines at the base and some spots of yellow, the posterior with a yellow bar; beneath the anterior are varied with black, yellow and red, and the posterior have alternate bars of red and yellow, with a slender black edge. Expanse of the wings, $1\frac{1}{2}$ inch.

SYN. Hesperia (U.) Propertius, *Fabr. Ent. Syst.* III. 1. *p.* 325. *Enc. Méth.* 9. 773.

HABITAT. "In India," (*Fabricius*).

HESPERIA TIBULLUS.

Plate XLVII. fig. 3.

SPECIES. HESPERIA TIBULLUS: alis supra anticis nigris flavo-maculatis; subtus subconcoloribus, costa subrufa; posticis flavis margine omni, postico interrupto, nigro, subtus variegatis. Expans. alar. unc. $1\frac{1}{2}$.

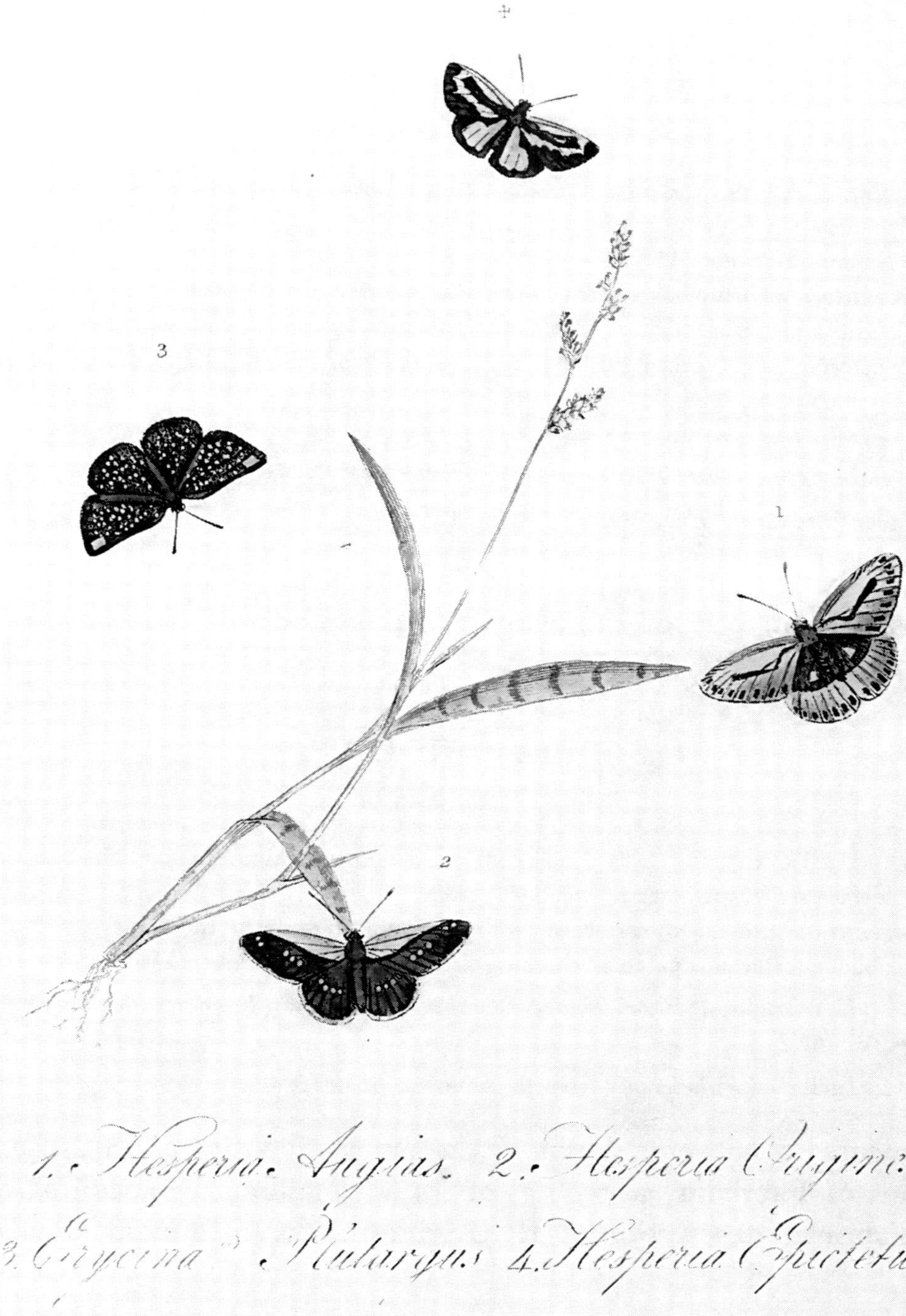

1. Hesperia Augias. 2. Hesperia Origines.
3. Erycina? Plutargus 4. Hesperia Epictetus.

LEPIDOPTERA.

HESPERIA: with the anterior wings above black, spotted with yellow; beneath similarly coloured, but with a reddish costa; posterior pair yellow with the margin (interrupted behind) black, beneath variegated. Expanse of the wings, 1½ inch.

SYN. Hesperia (U.) Tibullus, *Fabr. Ent. Syst.* III. 1. *p.* 326, *Enc. Méth.* 9. 754.

HABITAT. "In Indiis," (*Fabricius*).

HESPERIA AUGIAS.

Plate XLVIII. fig. 1.

SPECIES. HESPERIA AUGIAS: alis fulvis; supra anticis linea obliqua, limboque postico nigris; posticis nigris, puncto subcentrali fasciaque postica utrinque dentatis rufo-flavis. Expans. alar. unc. 1¼.

HESPERIA: with fulvous wings; above the anterior are marked by an oblique line, and the posterior edge of black; the posterior are black, with a central spot and a posterior bar, toothed on each side, of reddish yellow. Expanse of the wings, 1¼ inch.

SYN. Papilio (Pleb. Urb.) Augias, *Linn. Amœn. Acad. t.* 4, *p.* 410. *Syst. Nat.* 2. 794. *Fabr. Ent. Syst.* III. 1. *p.* 327. *Enc. Méth.* 9. 767, (Hesperia A.)

HABITAT. Java, (*Linnæus, Enc. Méth.*) India, (*Fabricius*).

The specimen here figured appears to be less strongly marked with black than ordinary, the posterior margin of the wings being spotted with that colour, instead of being entirely black.

HESPERIA ORIGINES.

Plate XLVIII. fig. 2.

SPECIES. HESPERIA ORIGINES: alis fuscis; striga punctorum alborum; anticis basi obliquè testaceis. Expans. alar. unc. 1¼.

HESPERIA: with the wings brown, with a row of white dots; the anterior with a large oblique testaceous patch at the base. Expanse of the wings, 1¼ inch.

SYN. Hesperia (U.) Origines, *Fabr. Ent. Syst.* III. 1. *p.* 328, (Hesperia Thaumas). *Enc. Méth.* 9. 766?

HABITAT. "In Indiis," (*Fabricius.*) North America, (*Enc. Méth.*)

As there appears to be some doubt of the precise identity of this insect with the Hesperia Thaumus of Fabricius, as well as of its sex, and as the accompanying figure agrees with the Fabrician description of H. Origines, I have thought it best to retain the latter name.

ERYCINA? PLUTARGUS.

Plate XLVIII. fig. 3.

SPECIES. ERYCINA? PLUTARGUS: alis supra fuscis auro irroratis, anticis macula apicali testacea; subtus pallidioribus, anticis margine exteriori testaceo, posticis strigis punctoque obscurioribus. Expans. alar. $1\frac{1}{8}$ unc.

ERYCINA? with the wings above brown with gold spangles, and with a testaceous spot at the tips of the anterior pair; beneath paler, the anterior with the front margin testaceous; the posterior pair with streaks and a spot of darker colour. Expanse of the wings, $1\frac{1}{8}$ inch.

SYN. Hesperia (U.) Plutargus, *Fab. Ent. Syst.* III. 1. *p.* 329. *Enc. Méth.* 9. 776 (Hesperia P.)

HABITAT. "In Indiis," (*Fabricius*).

HESPERIA EPICTETUS.

Plate XLVIII. fig. 4.

SPECIES. HESPERIA EPICTETUS: alis fuscis, disco flavo; anticarum macula longitudinali fusca et in hac lunula flava; posticis subtus flavis immaculatis. Expans. alar. unc. 1.

HESPERIA: with the wings brown, the disc being yellow; the anterior pair having a longitudinal brown spot running through the middle of the wing, in which is a yellow lunule; the posterior pair are yellow and without spots beneath. Expanse of the wings, 1 inch.

SYN. Hesperia (U.) Epictetus, *Fabr. Ent. Syst.* III. 1. *p.* 330. *Enc. Méth.* 9. 768.

HABITAT. "In Indiis, (*Fabricius*). Brazil, (*Enc. Méth.*)

HESPERIA CHEMNIS.

Plate XLIX. fig. 1.

SPECIES. HESPERIA CHEMNIS: alis subcaudatis, fuscis basi magis brunneis; anticis maculis sex, posticis tribus quadratis hyalinis, margine postico flavo. Expans. alar. unc. $2\frac{1}{2}$.

HESPERIA: with the wings slightly tailed, brown, with the base more fulvous; anterior pair with six, posterior with three square hyaline spots; posterior margin yellow. Expanse of the wings, $2\frac{1}{2}$ inches.

SYN. Hesperia (U.) Chemnis, *Fabr. Ent. Syst.* III. 1. *p.* 331. *Enc Méth.* 9. 746.

HABITAT. "In Indiis," (*Fabricius*).

1. Hesperia Chemnis. 2. Hesperia Thrax
3. H. Mithridates. 4. H. Thrasibulus.

HESPERIA THRAX.

Plate XLIX. fig. 2.

SPECIES. HESPERIA THRAX: alis ecaudatis, fuscis, maculis tribus fenestratis, exteriore minore. Expans. alar. unc. $2\frac{1}{2}$.

HESPERIA: without tails, with brown wings, the anterior having three fenestrated spots, of which the outer one is smallest. Expanse of the wings, $2\frac{1}{2}$ inches.

SYN. Papilio (Pl. Urb.) Thrax, *Linn. Syst. Nat.* 2. 794. *Enc. Méth.* 9. 748, (Hesperia T.) *Fabr. Ent. Syst.* III. 1. *p.* 337?

HABITAT. Java, (*Linnæus, Enc. Méth.*)

Donovan expressly states that his specimen of this insect corresponded with that in the Linnæan cabinet. It also agrees with the description of a Javanese butterfly described in the Encyclopédie Méthodique as the true Thrax. This circumstance renders doubtful the references to Fabricius, Clerk, and Cramer, who has figured three species, regarded as varieties of Thrax, under the names of Papilio Salus, Sebaldus, and Ramasis.

HESPERIA (EANTIS) MITHRIDATES.

Plate XLIX. fig. 3.

SUBGENUS. EANTIS, *Boisduval.*

SPECIES. HESPERIA (EANTIS) MITHRIDATES: alis atris, purpureo-maculatis, fasciaque submarginali purpurea lunulis albidis; subtus nigris fasciis duabus macularibus purpureis. Expans. alar. unc. 2.

HESPERIA (EANTIS): with the wings black, spotted with purple, and with a purple submarginal fascia, in which are whitish lunules; beneath black, with two rows of purple spots. Expanse of the wings, 2 inches.

SYN. Hesperia (U.) Mithridates, *Fabr. Ent. Syst.* III. 1. *p.* 336. *Enc. Méth.* 9. 792, (Hesperia M)

HABITAT. "In Indiis, (*Fabricius*). Brazil? (*Enc. Méth.*)

HESPERIA (EANTIS) THRASIBULUS.

Plate XLIX. fig. 4.

SPECIES. HESPERIA (EANTIS) THRASIBULUS: alis atris cæruleo undulatis; posticis subtus angulo ani cinereo fusco punctato. Expans. alar. unc. $1\frac{1}{2}$.

HESPERIA (EANTIS): with black wings, undulated with blue; the posterior beneath with the anal angle cinereous, spotted with brown. Expanse of the wings, $1\frac{1}{2}$ inch.

SYN. Hesperia (U.) Thrasibulus, *Fabr. Ent. Syst.* III. 1. *p.* 346. *Enc. Méth.* 9. 792.

HABITAT. "In Indiis," (*Fabricius*). Brazil, (*Enc. Méth.*)

HESPERIA JOVIANUS.

Plate L. fig. 1.

SPECIES. HESPERIA JOVIANUS: alis atris, anticis macula transversa pone medium (alteraque minori subapicali in ♀) alba, strigaque marginali punctorum oblongorum cæruleorum; posticis cæruleo striatis et in his maculæ aliquot oblongæ albæ. Expans. alar unc. $1\frac{1}{2}$.

HESPERIA: with the wings black; the anterior with a transverse bar of white beyond the middle, (a smaller subapical one in the female,) and a submarginal row of oblong blue dots; the posterior pair with blue streaks, in which are several oblong white spots. Expanse of the wings, $1\frac{1}{2}$ inch.

SYN. Hesperia (U.) Jovianus, *Fabricius Ent. Syst.* III. 1, *p.* 348. *Enc. Méth.* 9. 788.

HABITAT. "In Indiis," (*Fabricius.*) Brazil, (*Enc. Méth.*)

HESPERIA SALVIANUS.

Plate L. fig. 2.

SPECIES. HESPERIA SALVIANUS: alis supra fuscis, viridi maculatis strigaque postica macularum obscuriorum; subtus anticis fuscis fascia lata alba, posticis albis striga marginali e punctis septem fuscis. Expans. alar. unc. $1\frac{1}{2}$.

HESPERIA: with the upper side of the wings brown, mottled with green, and with a submarginal row of obscure dots; beneath the anterior wings brown with a broad white bar, posterior white with a marginal row of seven brown dots. Expanse of the wings, $1\frac{1}{2}$ inch.

SYN. Hesperia (U.) Salvianus, *Fabr. Ent. Syst.* III. 1. *p.* 348. *Enc. Méth.* 9. 789.

HABITAT. "In Indiis," (*Fabricius*).

1. Hesperia Jovianus. 2. H. Salvianus. 3. H. Galenu.
4. H. Catullus. 5. H. Spio.

HESPERIUS GALENUS.

Plate L. fig. 3.

SPECIES. HESPERIA GALENUS: alis fuscis punctis maculisque flavis; anticis fascia maculari transversa media; posticis macula magna oblonga e medio ad marginem extensa. Expans. alar. unc. $1\frac{1}{2}$.

HESPERIA: with the wings brown with yellow dots and spots; the anterior with a central transverse row of spots forming a bar, and the latter with a large oblong spot reaching from the middle to the tips. Expanse of the wings, $1\frac{1}{2}$ inch.

SYN. Hesperia (U.) Galenus, *Fabr. Ent. Syst.* III. 1, *p.* 350. *Enc. Méth.* 9. 773.

HABITAT. "In Indiis," (*Fabricius*).

HESPERIA CATULLUS.

Plate L. fig. 4.

SPECIES. HESPERIA CATULLUS: alis atris, striga communi submarginali punctorum alborum; anticis etiam punctis nonnullis albis, subtus paucioribus. Expans. alar. unc. $1\frac{1}{6}$.

HESPERIA: with the wings black, with a row of submarginal white dots on all the wings; the anterior pair have also a few white dots scattered over the surface, being fewer beneath. Expanse of the wings, $1\frac{1}{6}$ inch.

SYN. Hesperia (U.) Catullus, *Fabr. Ent. Syst.* III. 1, *p.* 348. *Abbot and Smith Lep. Georgia,* 1. *t.* 24. *Enc. Méth.* 9. 777.

HABITAT. "In Indiis," (*Fabricius*). North America, (*Abbot and Smith*).

According to the Encyclopédie Méthodique, this North American insect is liable to considerable variation in the number of the white dots on the upper surfaces of the wings. The caterpillar, according to Abbot and Smith, feeds upon the Monarda punctata. It is of a dark green colour, with two black spots on the first segment; the head is black, with two white dots at the sides.

HESPERIA SPIO.

Plate L. fig. 5.

SPECIES. HESPERIA SPIO: alis reversis, nigris, maculis albis plurimis difformibus undique dispersis, subtus simillimis at fuscis. "Similis P. Tages at dimidio minor et brevis."—*Linn.*

HESPERIA: with the wings reversed, black, with many irregular shaped white spots scattered over the wings; beneath exactly alike, but the black changed to brown. Similar to P. Tages, but smaller by half, and short.

SYN. Papilio (P. N.) Spio, *Linn. Mus. Ulr. p.* 338. (*nec* 330). *Syst. Nat.* 2. 796. *Fabr. Ent. Syst.* III. 1. *p.* 354.

HABITAT. Cape of Good Hope, (*Linnæus*). India, (*Fabricius*).

Linnæus, both in the Museum Reginæ Ulricæ, and the Systema Naturæ, states that he received this from the Cape of Good Hope, from Tulbagh, who was governor there. I know not upon what authority Fabricius gave it as a native of India.

The five preceding species are represented on the Clerodendrum infortunatum, a plant introduced from the East Indies.

HESPERIA ENNIUS.

Plate LI. fig. 1.

SPECIES. HESPERIA ENNIUS: alis anticis fuscis, maculis hyalinis; posticis supra atris, macula magna media, maculisque marginalibus flavis; subtus fuscis nigro maculatis discoque albo. Expans. alar. unc. $2\frac{1}{10}$.

HESPERIA: with the anterior wings brown, with hyaline spots; the posterior above black, with a large central spot, (extending to the base,) and marginal spots of yellow; beneath brown, spotted with black, and with the disc white. Expanse of the wings, $2\frac{1}{10}$ inches.

SYN. Hesperia (U.) Ennius, *Fabr. Ent. Syst.* III. 1, *p.* 338. *Enc. Méth.* 9. 749.

HABITAT. "In Indiis," (*Fabricius*).

HESPERIA POLYBIUS.

Plate LI. fig. 2.

SPECIES. HESPERIA POLYBIUS: alis concoloribus; anticis atris, macula media transversa fulva, margine postico niveo; posticis atris, margine postico niveo, anguloque ani fulvo. Expans. alar. unc. $2\frac{1}{4}$.

HESPERIA: with the wings coloured alike on both sides; anterior pair black, with a transverse central fulvous spot, posterior margin white; posterior wings with the margin white and anal angle fulvous. Expanse of the wings, $2\frac{1}{4}$ inches.

SYN. Hesperia (U.) Polybius, *Fabr. Ent. Syst.* III. 1. *p.* 337. *Enc. Méth.* 9. 732.
Hesperia (U.) Palemon, *Fabr. Ent. Syst.* III. 1, *p.* 335. *Sp. Ins.* 2. 134. *Cramer, pl.* 131. *F.*

HABITAT. "In Indiis, (*Fabricius.*) Surinam, Brazil, (*Enc. Méth.*)

1. *Hesperia Ennius.* 2. *Hesperia Polybius.*
3. *Hesperia Teleucus.*

1. Hesperia Orcus. 2. Hesperia Busiris.

3. Hesperia Celsus.

LEPIDOPTERA.

HESPERIA ZELEUCUS.

Plate LI. fig. 3.

SPECIES. HESPERIA ZELEUCUS: atra, capite anoque sanguineis; alis concoloribus atris; posticis margine tenuissimo albo. Expans. alar. unc. 2¼.

HESPERIA: black, with the head and anus sanguineous; wings coloured alike on both sides, black; the posterior with a very slender white margin. Expanse of the wings, 2¼ inches.

SYN. Hesperia (U.) Zeleucus, *Fabr. Ent. Syst.* III. 1. *p.* 346. *Enc. Meth.* 9. 733.
Papilio Thasus, *Cramer, pl.* 380, *f. M, N.*

HABITAT. "In Indiis," (*Fabricius*). Surinam, and Brazil, (*Enc. Méth.*)

The three preceding species are represented on a sprig of the Lagerstrœmeria Indica.

HESPERIA ORCUS.

Plate LII. fig. 1.

SPECIES. HESPERIA ORCUS: alis subtus fuscis, anticis punctis maculaque lunata vitreo-flavis; posticis fasciis obsoletis cæruleis; subtus cærulescentibus, margine nigro. Expans. alar. unc. 1½.

HESPERIA: with the wings above brown, the anterior with several spots, and a lunate mark of glassy yellow, the posterior with obsolete blue bars; beneath blue with a black edge. Expanse of the wings, 1½ inch.

SYN. Hesperia (U.) Orcus, *Fabr. Ent. Syst.* III, 1. *p.* 341 *Enc. Méth.* 9. 789.
Papilio Cerialis, *Cramer Pap. pl.* 392, *fig. N, O. Stoll Suppl. Cramer, pl.* 10, *fig.* 1.

HABITAT. "In Indiis," (*Fabricius*). Guiana, (*Enc. Méth. Stoll.*)

The caterpillar, according to Stoll, (who observed the transformations of this species in Guiana,) is dirty green, with the head brown, a spot on each side of the segments of the body, and two ventral lines of white. It remains in the chrysalis state only about seven days.

HESPERIA BUSIRIS.

Plate LII. fig. 2.

SPECIES. HESPERIA BUSIRIS: thorace albo punctato; alis anticis oblongis, atris, maculis duabus, et inter has punctis duobus flavis, apice cinerascente; posticis fulvis margine atro. Expans. alar. unc. 2.

HESPERIA: with the thorax spotted with white; the anterior wings oblong, black, with two large spots, between which are two dots of yellow, the tip being cinereous; the posterior wings fulvous, with a black margin. Expanse of the wings, 2 inches.

SYN. Hesperia (U,) Busiris, *Fabr. Ent. Syst.* III. 1, *p.* 345. *Enc. Méth.* 9. 758.

HABITAT. "In India," (*Fabricius*).

HESPERIA CELSUS.

Plate LII. fig. 3.

SPECIES. HESPERIA CELSUS: alis supra nigris, subtus brunneo-fuscis; anticis utrinque fascia transversa rufo-flavida; posticis supra immaculatis, infra cinerascenti-pulverulentis, margine externo strigaque transversa brunneo-fuscis. Expans. alar. unc. 1¾.

HESPERIA: with the wings above black, beneath rich brown; the anterior on both sides with a transverse fascia of reddish yellow; the posterior pair immaculate above, beneath sprinkled ashy, with the outer margin and a transverse bar rich brown. Expanse of the wings, 1¾ inch.

SYN. Hesperia (U.) Celsus, *Fabr. Ent. Syst.* III. 1. *p.* 346. *Enc. Méth.* 9. 759.
Papilio Hiarbas, *Cramer, pl.* 18, *fig. F?*
Hesperia (U.) Thyrsis, *Fabr. Ent. Syst.* III. 1, *p.* 333?

HABITAT. "In Indiis," (*Fabricius.*) Brazil, (*Enc. Méth.*)

ZEUZERA MINEA.

Plate LIII. fig. 1, male. 1 *a*, female.

SECTION. LEPIDOPTERA Nocturna. Phalæna, *Linnæus.*

FAMILY. HEPIALIDÆ, *Leach.*

GENUS. ZEUZERA, *Latreille, Stephens.*

SPECIES. ZEUZERA MINEA: cyanea, alis concoloribus aurantiis, maculis fasciaque media longitudinali cyaneis. Expans. alar. unc. 3—4.

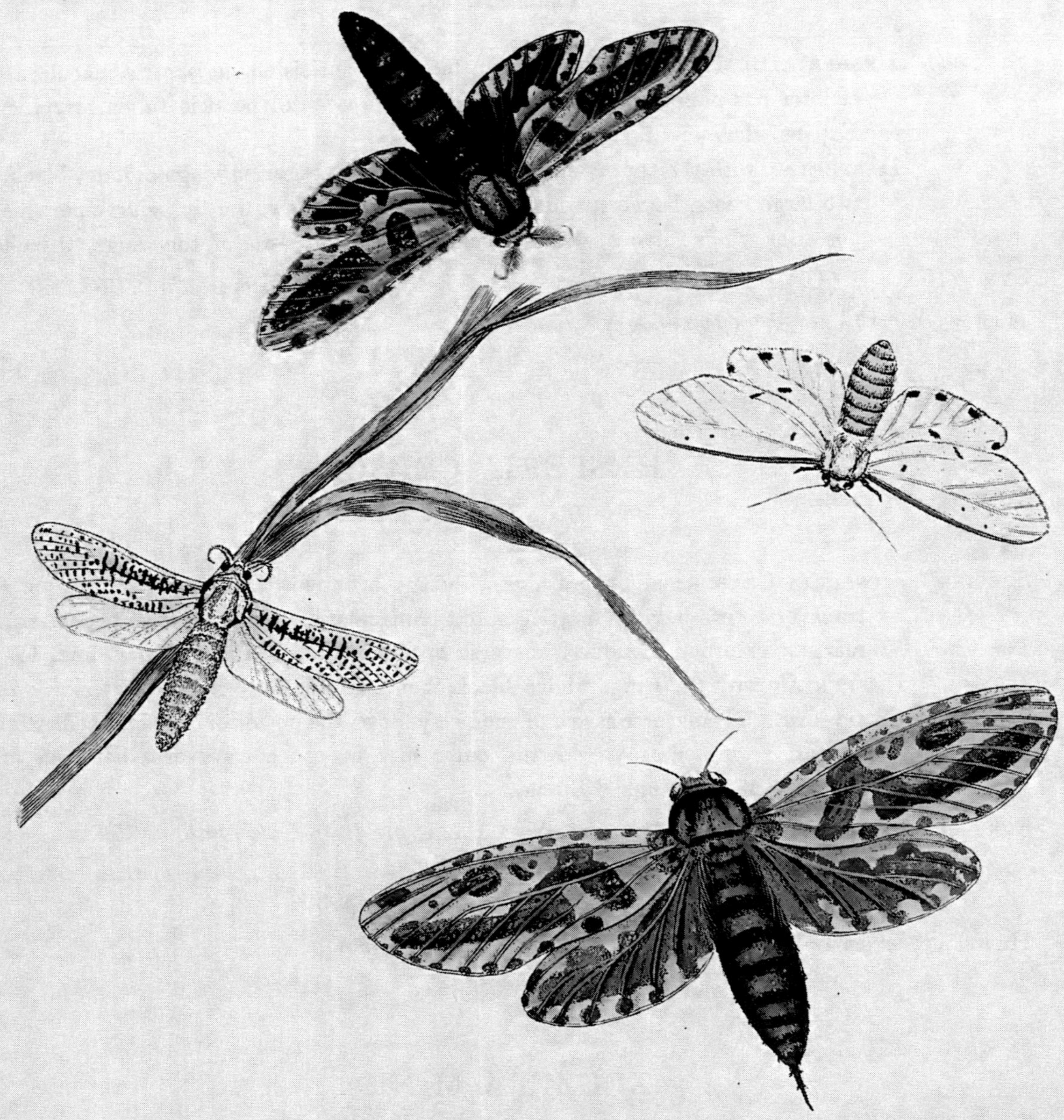

1. *Zeuzera Mineas.* 2 *Zeuzera scalaris.*

3 *Lithosia sanguinolenta.*

LEPIDOPTERA.

ZEUZERA: cyaneous, with all the wings coloured alike, orange, with cyaneous spots, and a broad central longitudinal bar of the same colour. Expanse of the wings, from 3 to 4 inches.

Donovan observes that "Cramer has given the figure of a small specimen of this fine Phalæna under the trivial name of Mineus. This is evidently of the male; the antennæ of which are not, however, very correctly expressed. Both sexes of this rare insect are represented in the annexed plate, the drawings of which were taken from specimens met with in Bengal, by Mr. Fichtel of Vienna. The originals are at this time in the cabinet of the Emperor of Germany." The same insect, but apparently from a very indifferent specimen, is figured by Eschscholtz in Kotzebue's Entdeckungs Reise in die Sud. see, &c. Weimar, 1821, *p.* 219, *pl.* 11, *fig.* 29, under the name of Zeuzera viridicans.

ZEUZERA SCALARIS.

Plate LIII. fig. 2.

SPECIES. ZEUZERA SCALARIS: nivea; thorace utrinque linea fulva; alis niveis, anticis strigis numerosissimis transversalibus abbreviatis nigris, striaque longitudinali fulva, posticis immaculatis. Expans. alar. unc. $2\frac{1}{4}$.

ZEUZERA: snow-white; the thorax on each side with a fulvous line; wings snow-white, the anterior with many short transverse black lines and a fulvous longitudinal line, the posterior immaculate. Expanse of the wings, $2\frac{1}{4}$ inches.

SYN. Cossus scalaris, *Fabr. Ent. Syst.* III. 1. *p.* 5. *Mant. Ins.* 2. *p.* 135, (Hepialus s.)

Described by Fabricius, from a specimen in the cabinet of Mr. Monson, as a native of China. The specimen represented in the annexed plate was brought from Bengal, and is, as well as the preceding, at this time in the cabinet of the Emperor of Austria.

LITHOSIA SANGUINOLENTA.

Plate LIII. fig. 3.

FAMILY. LITHOSIIDÆ, *Stephens.*

GENUS. LITHOSIA, *Fabricius.* Callimorpha p. *Latreille.*

SPECIES. LITHOSIA SANGUINOLENTA: alis incumbentibus, niveis, anticis costa sanguinea, per thoracis partem anticam ducta, posticis maculis atris; abdomine fulvo annulis nigris. Expans. alar. $2\frac{1}{3}$ unc.

LITHOSIA: with the wings incumbent, snow white; the anterior with the front edge sanguineous, which is carried across the front of the thorax; posterior pair spotted with black; abdomen fulvous with black rings. Expanse of the wings, $2\frac{1}{8}$ inches.

SYN. Bombyx sanguinolenta, *Fabr. Ent. Syst.* III. 1. *p.* 473.

Donovan observes that this is a rare species, and that his specimen was received from Bombay.

PSILURA FIGURA.

Plate LIV. fig. 1.

FAMILY. ARCTIIDÆ, *Stephens.* Phalæna, (Bombyx p.) *Linnæus.*

GENUS. PSILURA, *Stephens.* Liparis p. *Ochs.* Laria p. *Schrank.*

SPECIES. PSILURA FIGURA: alis anticis albidis, fusco nigroque maculatis, medio figura 7 nigra notatis; posticis cinereis; abdomine carneo. Expans. alar. unc. $3\frac{1}{8}$.

PSILURA: with the anterior wings whitish, spotted with brown and black, and marked in the middle with a black character like the figure 7; posterior wings cinereous; abdomen pink. Expanse of the wings, $3\frac{1}{8}$ inches.

Donovan states that he received this nondescript species from Madras. As it agrees with our common moth, the black arches (Ps. Monacha) in its general character, and in the peculiar pink colouring of the abdomen, I have placed it in the genus of which that species is the type. In the markings of the wings, however, it seems to make a nearer approach to the tussock moths.

OPHIUSA? STRIGATA.

Plate LIV. fig. 2.

FAMILY. NOCTUIDÆ, *Stephens.* Phalæna, (Noctua) *Linnæus.*

GENUS. OPHIUSA? *Ochs. Tr. Steph.* Ophideres? *Boisduval Faune de l'Oceanie, p.* 245.

SPECIES. OPHIUSA STRIGATA: "alis anticis fuscis, litura longitudinali viridi; posticis luteis, lunula limboque nigris." (*Donovan*). Expans. alar. unc. 3.

1. Psilura figura. 2. Ophiusa strigata
3. Erebus hieroglyphicus.

OPHIUSA: with the "anterior wings brown, with a longitudinal green daub; posterior pair yellowish, with a lunar spot and border of black." Expanse of the wings, 3 inches.

Donovan observes that "this moth agrees entirely with the Noctua Dioscoreæ of Fabricius, (*Ent. Syst. t.* 3, *p.* 2, *p.* 16, *n.* 26.) except in having a large green streak on the upper wings. It appears, indeed, to have been hitherto confounded with that species, either as a sexual difference, or variety; but we are persuaded it is neither. Both sexes of N. Dioscoreæ, in particular, have occurred to our observation, without this streak. Found in Bengal." It should be observed, however, that Fabricius, not only in this, but also in the allied species Materna, (figured by Drury, *vol.* 2, *t.* 13.) states that the colour of the anterior wings is liable to great variation. The emargination of the posterior margin of the fore wings in this figure, is also noticed by Fabricius under Dioscoreæ, and is probably a sexual character.

EREBUS HIEROGLYPHICUS.

Plate LIV. fig. 3.

GENUS. EREBUS, *Latreille.* Thysania, *Dalm.* Noctua, *Fabricius.*

SPECIES. EREBUS HIEROGLYPHICUS: alis dentatis, atris; anticis fascia subapicali abbreviata albida maculaque subocellari; posticis margine bisinuato. Expans. alar. unc. $3\frac{1}{4}$—$\frac{1}{2}$.

EREBUS: with the wings dentated, black; the anterior with a short whitish line near the tip, and a large central ocellated spot; the posterior immaculate with two deep notches. Expanse of the wings, $3\frac{1}{4}$—$\frac{1}{2}$ inches.

SYN. Phalæna (Noctua) hieroglyphica, *Drury App. vol.* 2, *pl.* 2, *fig.* 1. *Oliv. Enc. Méth.* 8. 253. *Fabr. Ent. Syst.* III. 2. *p.* 11.

Phalæna Magdonia, *Cramer Pap. pl.* 174, *fig. F.*

"Common in the East Indies."—*Donovan.*

Order. NEUROPTERA, *Linnæus.*

MYRMELEON PARDALIS.

Plate LV. fig. 1.

SECTION. PLANIPENNES, *Latreille.* (Filicornes.)

FAMILY. MYRMELEONIDÆ, *Leach.*

GENUS. MYRMELEON, *Linn.* &c.

SPECIES. MYRMELEON PARDALIS: alis albis, maculis plurimis nigris sparsis, pedibus nigris femoribus flavis, corpore flavo nigroque vario. Expans. alar. unc. $3\frac{1}{4}$.

MYRMELEON: with the wings white, with many black dots scattered over them, especially in the anterior pair; legs black, with the thighs yellow; body varied with yellow and black. Expanse of the wings, $3\frac{1}{4}$ inches.

SYN. Myrmeleon Pardalis, *Fabr. Ent. Syst.* 2. *p.* 92.

MYRMELEON PUNCTATUM.

Plate LV. fig. 2.

SPECIES. MYRMELEON PUNCTATUM: alis hyalino-albidis, venis e punctis niveis nigrisque alternis reticulatis, punctoque magno niveo stigmaticali; pedibus flavescentibus. Expans. alar. unc. $2\frac{1}{4}$.

MYRMELEON: with the wings hyaline whitish, with the veins reticulated alternately with black and white, and with a large white stigmal spot, legs yellowish. Expanse of the wings, $2\frac{1}{4}$ inches.

SYN. Myrmeleon Punctatum, *Fabr. Ent. Syst.* 2, *p.* 94.

Donovan observes upon the two preceding species—" Few species of the Myrmeleon genus have been discovered. Linnæus describes only five, and those are chiefly natives of Europe. Fabricius adds seven more, besides three others in the genera Ascalaphus, in the Entomologia Systematica, and particularly two from India, in the cabinet of Sir Joseph Banks, Bart. M. Pardalis and M. Punctatum; these are the only Indian Myrmeleons hitherto ascertained; to the Entomologist they are equally interesting as new and unfigured species, but M. Pardalis is much superior in beauty to the other. The characteristic distinction of M. Punctatum, is the alternate black and white specks, or interrupted dashes in the reticulations of the wings. M. Pardalis is

1

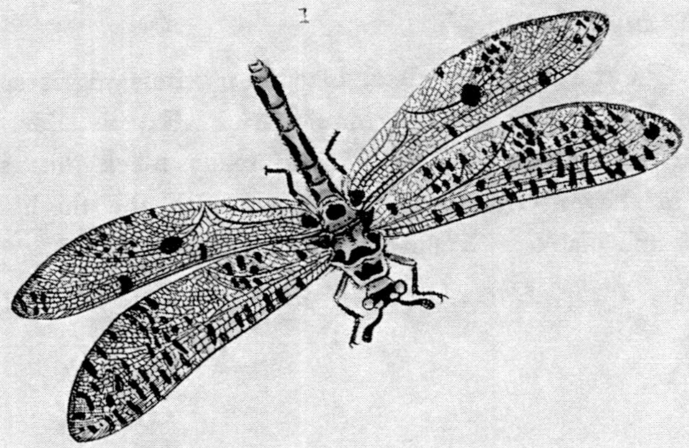

2

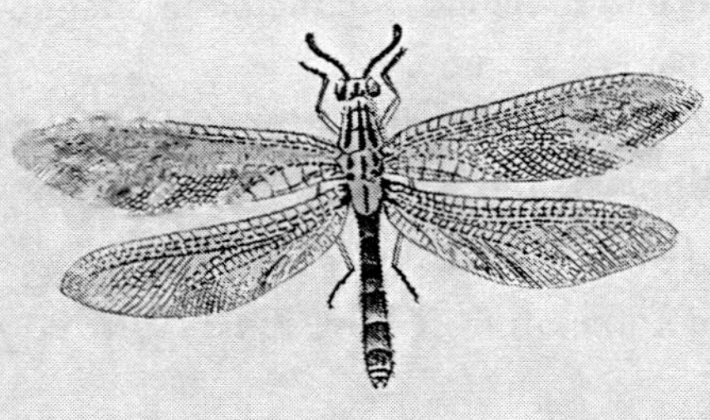

1. Myrmeleon Pardalis. 2. Myrmeleon punctatum

1. Chrysis imperialis
2. Stilbum oculatum. 3. Stilbum splendidum

reticulated also with delicate brownish nerves, its general colour a fine yellow, elegantly barred with transverse streaks of brown; it is from the coast of Coromandel."

The natural history of the Myrmeleon-larva is curious, and has been traced in some of the European kinds by Reaumur, Roesel, and others, particularly in the M. Formica-Leo of Geoffroy; this creature, among other peculiarities, is furnished in the front with a large pair of forceps, with which it takes its prey. It forms circular cavities in the sand, and concealing itself in the centre with only the forceps above the surface, catches the weaker or unwary insects that come within the verge of its cell.

Order. HYMENOPTERA, *Linnæus.*

CHRYSIS IMPERIALIS.

Plate LVI. fig. 1.

SECTION. TUBULIFERA, *Latreille.*

FAMILY. CHRYSIDIDÆ, *Leach.*

GENUS. CHRYSIS, *Linnæus.*

SPECIES. CHRYSIS IMPERIALIS: "thorace viridi, fascia cyanea; abdomine antice cyaneo violaceoque fasciato, medio aureo, postice rubro, quadri-dentato."—*Donovan.* Long. Corp. $\frac{5}{8}$ unc.

CHRYSIS: with the thorax green, with a blue band; anterior part of the abdomen blue fasciated with violet, golden in the middle, posterior end red, with four teeth. Length of the body, $\frac{5}{8}$ of an inch.

SYN. Chrysis fasciata, *Donovan,* 1*st edit. nec* Chrysis fasciata, *Fabr. Syst. Piez. p.* 175.

"This charming insect is from Tranquebar, where we have every reason to believe it to be uncommonly rare. The species does not appear to be described by any author, the only specimen we are acquainted with, is in the cabinet of the Right Hon. Sir J. Banks, Bart."—*Donovan.*

This species must not be confounded with the Chrysis fasciata of Fabricius, a

South American species, for which it will be convenient to retain the specific name of C. fasciata, (especially as it is now impossible to decide the priority of the employment of the name fasciata between Fabricius or Donovan, both having been published in the year 1804.) I have, therefore, proposed for Donovan's insect a name, which will not be thought inapplicable.

STILBUM OCULATUM.

Plate LVI. fig. 2.

GENUS. STILBUM, *Spinola.* Chrysis p. *Fabricius, Donovan.*

SPECIES. STILBUM OCULATUM: viride, nitens, punctatum; abdomine rotundato, viride, versus apicem utrinque macula ocellata aurea; ano cæruleo sex-dentato. Long. Corp. unc. $\frac{1}{2}$.

STILBUM: green, shining, punctured; abdomen rounded above, green, with an eye-like golden spot on each side near the tip; anus blue with six teeth. Length of the body, $\frac{1}{2}$ an inch.

SYN. Chrysis oculata, *Fabr. Ent. Syst.* 2, *p.* 239. *Sp. Ins. p.* 455. *Syst. Piez. p.* 171.

"Chrysis oculata is distinguished for the peculiar brilliancy of its colours. It was found by Dr. Kœnig at Tranquebar. Fabricius describes this insect from a specimen in the collection of Sir Joseph Banks, Bart.; from whence our figure is also taken. We have since received the same kind from Bengal, through the medium of Mr. Fichtel of Vienna."—*Donovan.*

STILBUM SPLENDIDULUM.

Plate LVI. fig. 3.

SPECIES. STILBUM SPLENDIDULUM: viride, cyaneo nitidum; abdomine rotundato; ano cæruleo quadri-dentato; pedibus viridibus, tibiis fuscis. Long. Corp. $\frac{9}{10}$ unc.

STILBUM: green, shining with blue; abdomen rounded above; anus blue, with four teeth; legs green, with brown tibiæ. Length of the body, $\frac{9}{10}$ of an inch.

SYN. Chrysis splendidula, *Fabr. Sp. Ins. p.* 454. *Ent. Syst.* II. *p.* 238. *Syst. Piez. p.* 170.

Donovan states that this species is "very scarce, and that it is a native of Tranquebar, where it was discovered by Dr. Kœnig. Fabricius describes this insect from a specimen in the cabinet of Sir Joseph Banks, Bart. A variety of the same

1. *Vespa cincta*. 2. *Eumenes petiolata*. 3. *E. arcuata*. 4. *Polistes*. *Macaensis*. 5. *P. tepida*. 6. *Xylocopa nasalis*.

species is found in New Holland." It is most probable that the Australasian specimens constitute a distinct but very closely allied species. The Stilbum princeps of G. R. Gray, figured in Griffith's Animal Kingdom, Insects, *pl.* 77, from the collection of the Rev. F. W. Hope, is from Melville Island, and is perhaps identical with the New Holland variety, mentioned by Fabricius and Donovan.

VESPA CINCTA.

Plate LVII. fig. 1.

SECTION. ACULEATA, *Latreille.*

FAMILY. VESPIDÆ, *Leach.*

GENUS. VESPA, *Linnæus.*

SPECIES. VESPA CINCTA: nigra; capite nigro; thorace maculato scutelloque obscuro, fulvis; abdomine atro fascia ferruginea; alis ferrugineis, basi nigris. Long. Corp. unc. 1.

VESPA: black, with the head black; thorax with two spots on each side before the wings, and the scutellum obscure fulvous; abdomen black, with a ferruginous or fulvous bar; wings ferruginous; black at the base. Length of the body, 1 inch.

SYN. Vespa cincta, *Fabr. Ent. Syst.* 2. *p.* 253. *Syst. Piez. p.* 253. *St. Fargeau Hist. Nat. Hymenopt.* 1. *p.* 505.

Sphex tropica, *Sulzer Hist. Ins. tab.* 27, *fig.* 5.

Either this species is subject to considerable variation in its colours, or (which appears to me to be the case,) several distinct species have been confounded together under the name of V. cincta. Fabricius describes V. cincta from Tranquebar with the characters which I have abstracted above, adding a variety from the Cape of Good Hope, and a species under the name of V. affinis, being, as he says, "Nimis affinis V. cinctæ." M. le Comte de Saint Fargeau has also described two other varieties, under the name of cincta, neither of which precisely agree with the Fabrician character.

EUMENES PETIOLATA.

Plate LVII. fig. 2.

GENUS. EUMENES, *Latreille*.

SPECIES. EUMENES PETIOLATA: capite ferrugineo fascia verticali nigra; thorace ferrugineo, antice flavo; petiolo ferrugineo, basi fasciaque subapicali nigris, utrinque dente parvo armato; segmento secundo abdominis fascia atra, reliquis flavescentibus. Long. Corp. unc. $1\frac{1}{8}$.

EUMENES: with the head ferruginous, with a black vertical line; thorax ferruginous, pale yellow in front; petiole ferruginous, with the base and a band near the tip black, armed on each side with a small tooth; second abdominal segment with a black band, the remaining segments yellowish. Length of the body, $1\frac{1}{8}$ inch.

SYN. Vespa petiolata, *Fabr. Ent. Syst.* 2. *p.* 278. *Syst. Piez. p.* 284.

Donovan states that "this, with the foregoing species, is remarkably common in many parts of the East Indies. Fabricius speaks of it as a native of Malabar." The Chinese Vespa conica of Fabricius does not appear to be specifically distinct from the present species.

EUMENES ARCUATA.

Plate LVII. fig. 3.

SPECIES. EUMENES ARCUATA: nigra, fronte orbituque oculorum flavis; thorace flavo maculato et sub scutello flavo, cruce nigra notato; petiolo elongato incurvo atro, maculis duabus mediis et duabus ante apicem flavis; segmento secundo abdominis fasciis duabus, reliquis unica, interruptis flavis. Long. Corp. $1\frac{1}{8}$ unc.

EUMENES: black, with the face and the edges of the eyes yellow; thorax with yellow spots, behind the scutellum yellow with a black cross; petiole long, incurved, black, with two spots at the middle and two near the tips of yellow; second abdominal segment with two bands, the remainder with one, all being interrupted in the middle and yellow. Length of the body, $1\frac{1}{8}$ inch.

SYN. Vespa armata, *Fabr. Ent. Syst.* 2. *p.* 276. *Syst. Piez. p.* 287.

"Described by Fabricius as a native of New Holland; we have received it Madras."—*Donovan*.

HYMENOPTERA.

POLISTES MACAENSIS.

Plate LVII. fig. 4.

GENUS. POLISTES, *Latreille.*

SPECIES. POLISTES MACAENSIS: capite flavo, inter oculos nigro; thorace flavo, dorso obscururo, lineis tribus nigris; scutello flavo bilineato; aodomine flavo strigis tribus undatis. Long. Corp. unc. 1.

POLISTES: with the head yellow, black between the eyes; thorax yellow, darker above, with three black longitudinal lines; scutellum yellow, with two transverse lines; abdomen yellow, with three waved black transverse lines. Length of the body, 1 inch.

SYN. Vespa Macaensis, *Fabr. Ent. Syst.* 2. *p.* 259. *Syst. Piez. p.* 272.

"The specimen from which our figure is copied, is in the cabinet of the Right Hon. Sir J. Banks, Bart., from Macao."—*Donovan.* It is also very common in China, and appears to be the species so frequently represented in the drawings sent to this country, together with its nest, which is attached to the twigs of trees, and is composed of cells without any outer covering.

POLISTES TEPIDA.

Plate LVII. fig. 5.

SPECIES. POLISTES TEPIDA: capite nigro; labro ferrugineo; thorace nigro; collare punctisque duobus magnis dorsalibus ferrugineis; abdominis segmento primo nigro, secundo et tertio nigris, margine ferrugineo, reliquis totis ferrugineis. Long. Corp. $\frac{9}{10}$ unc.

POLISTES: with the head black; upper lip ferruginous; thorax black; collar and two large dorsal spots ferruginous; first segment of abdomen black, second and third black with the margin ferruginous, the remainder entirely ferruginous. Length of the body, $\frac{9}{10}$ths of an inch.

SYN. Vespa tepida, *Fabr. Ent. Syst.* 2. *p.* 262. *Syst. Piez. p.* 271.

Fabricius gives as the habitat of this insect, "Nova Hollandia, *Mus. Dom. Banks.*"

XYLOCOPA NASALIS. ♀.

Plate LVII. fig. 6.

FAMILY. APIDÆ, *Leach.*

GENUS. XYLOCOPA, *Fabricius.* Apis p. *Linnæus.*

SPECIES. XYLOCOPA NASALIS: nigra, nitida; subtus pedibusque hirsutissimis; alis nigris, purpureo (ad basin), viridique (ad apicem); nitentibus, facie sub antennas in fœmina alba. Long. Corp. $1\frac{1}{4}$ unc.

XYLOCOPA: black, shining; under side of the body and the legs very hairy; wings black, shining with purple at the base, and green towards the tips; the nose white in the female. Length of the body, $1\frac{1}{4}$ inch.

SYN. Xylocopa violacea, *Donovan,* 1*st edit.*

Donovan appears to have been in doubt as to the propriety of considering this very common Chinese insect as identical with the south of Europe X. violacea, *Linnæus,* with which it has hitherto been confounded. It is, however, much more elongated than that species, and is distinguished by the white nose of the female, whence I have proposed for it the specific name of X. nasalis.

Order. **DIPTERA,** *Linnæus.*

DIOPSIS INDICA.

Plate LVIII.

FAMILY. MUSCIDÆ, *Leach.*

GENUS. DIOPSIS, *Linnæus.*

SPECIES. DIOPSIS INDICA: ferruginea, oculis, thorace toto, abdomine postice, alraum macula apicali, spinisque scutellaribus nigris. Long. Corp. lin. 4. Expans. alar. lin. 6.

DIOPSIS: ferruginous, with the eyes, thorax, posterior part of the abdomen, terminal spot on the wings, and scutellar spines black. Length of the body, 4 lines. Expanse of the wings, 6 lines.

PL.

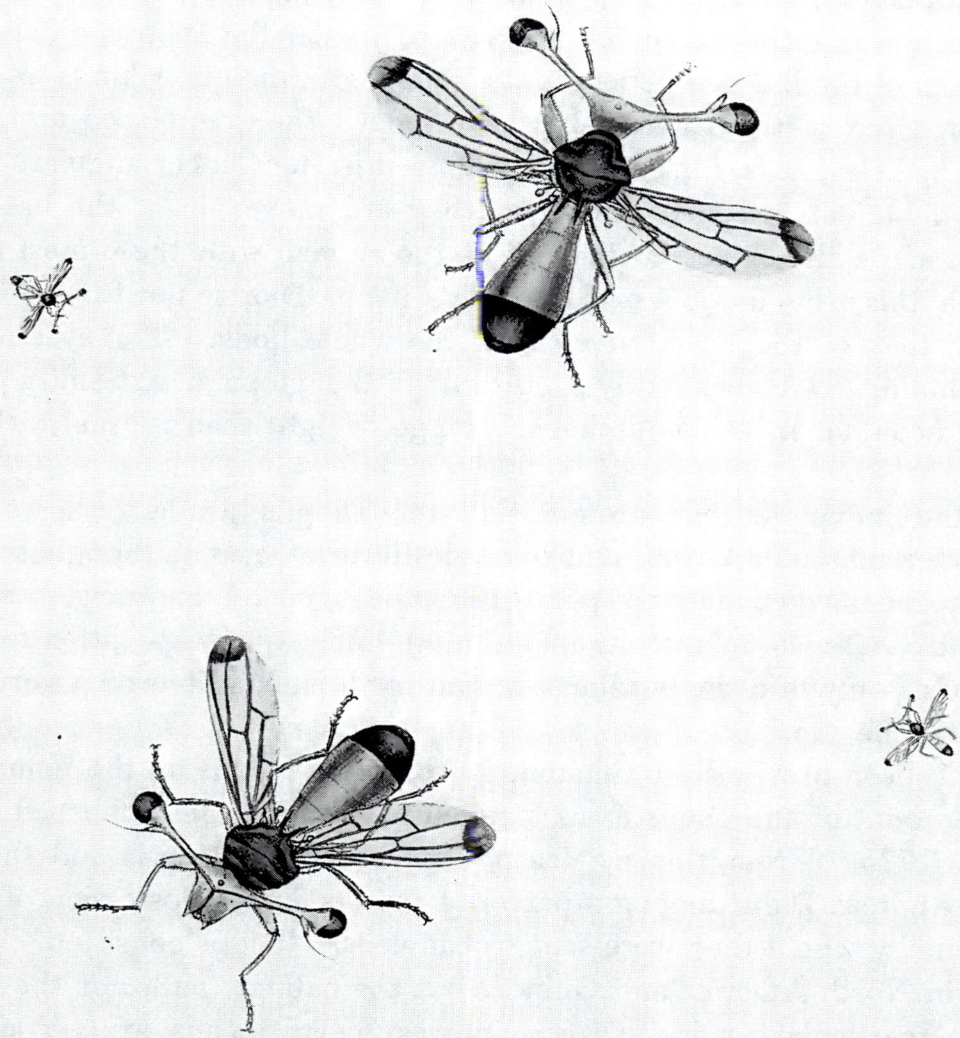

Diopsis Indica

SYN. Diopsis Indica, *Westw. in Trans. Soc. Linn. vol.* 17, *p.* 299.
Diopsis Ichneumonea, *Donovan*, 1*st edit.*

The appearance of this curious insect is peculiarly striking. Nothing can be more singular than the disposition of the eyes, which are situated at the extremity of two long immoveable pedicles arising from the head, most exactly in that part which in other insects bears the antennæ. In this particular the Diopsis differs not only from other insects of the kindred genera, but also from all the other kinds we are acquainted with. Some few of the Cancri, &c. have indeed the eyes placed at the extremity of elongated pedicles, as is, for example, instanced in the Cancer angulatus, yet these are obviously dissimilar in construction, for they are moveable at the base, and may be directed towards any object, at the will of the animal, with the utmost facility; but to accomplish this, the motion of the pedicle in the Diopsis must be necessarily accompanied by that of the head, or even of the whole body. The eyes of the latter are notwithstanding so conveniently stationed at the globular extremity of the pedicles, as to embrace a far more comprehensive range of sight than is usual with the generality of insects.

To the inexperienced entomologist, the Diopsis would rather seem to be furnished with remarkable horns, and to be destitute of eyes, although the latter are so very conspicuous when they are pointed out; it is, on the contrary, the true horns, or antennæ, that are so minute as to be most likely to escape attention, for each of these consists only of a single setaceous hair, or bristle, seated on a very small tubercle just beneath the eye.

It has been previously intimated, in the observations on the genus Paussus, that the first account of the Diopsis was inserted in a small tract published by Linnæus, at Upsal, in 1775. From this we learn, that both the Diopsis and the Paussus were found by Andreas Dahl, among a parcel of insects in the possession of Dr. Fothergill, of London, by whom they were sent to Linnæus. These consisted chiefly of insects collected in North America and Guinea, but the habitat, either of the Paussus, or the Diopsis in particular, it is very certain was by no means exactly known. Fuessly notwithstanding describes the D. ichneumonea, upon this ambiguous authority only, as a native of Cayenne, and after him Gmelin notes the same insect from South America, and Guinea, perhaps with as little reason. Latreille tells us it is from the coast of Angola, on the information of Perrin, a zealous naturalist of Bordeaux. Donovan's specimens of the insects here figured, and which he says are most assuredly the Diopsis ichneumonea of Linnæus, were brought from Bengal, where they were discovered by Mr. Fichtel, who, he adds, has thus established the habitat of this singular creature beyond dispute.

Linnæus, to whom only an individual species of Diopsis was known, as usual with him under such circumstances, does not assign to it any specific character. Donovan states that he was acquainted with another species of this genus, a native of Africa, in the collection of T. Marsham, Esq. which rendered a deviation from his example excusable, although the latter was at the time undescribed.

Since the preceding observations by Donovan was written, great additions have been made to this curious genus. Fabricius, like Donovan, adopted the Linnæan specific name ichneumonea, but confounded under that name two species distinct from each other, and from the original species. Illiger added another species, D. nigra. Dalman described three new African species; Weidemann another, which he named in honour of Dalman; and Gray another, D. Sykesii, in Griffith's Animal Kingdom. More recently, in the seventeenth volume of the Transactions of the Linnæan Society, I have published a monograph upon the genus, in which I have described thirty-one species, giving coloured figures of the greater portion. All of these species, (with the exception of D. brevicornis of Say, which belongs to a distinct subgenus,) are natives of the old world, inhabiting Guinea, Sierra Leone, Senegal, the Cape of Good Hope, Arabia, and the East Indies.

In this monograph I have endeavoured to prove, that Guinea, or the adjacent parts of Western Africa, is the true locality of D. ichneumonea; whilst Donovan's species, which belongs to a distinct section of the genus with the spot on the wings terminal, (and not merely a sub-apical fascia, as in D. ichneumonea,) I have given as a distinct species, under the name of D. Indica.

ALPHABETICAL INDEX.

In this Index, the names employed both in the present and former editions are introduced, in order to render the references which have been made by writers to the former edition available. The names, generic, subgeneric, or specific, first employed in the present edition, are distinguished by a *.

SYSTEMATIC INDEX.

INSECTA.

I.—MOUTH WITH JAWS.

II.—MOUTH SUCTORIAL.

Order. LEPIDOPTERA.

Family. Papilionidæ.

Family. Heliconiidæ.

Family. Nymphalidæ.

Family. Lycænidæ.

J. DAVY, Printer, Queen Street, Seven Dials.